# WOMEN IN AMERICAN SOCIETY

## An Historical Contribution

The rise and fall of concern for women's history has followed the course of the women's movement. Not since 1920, when the campaign for woman suffrage ended, has there been the interest evident today. Once again women are looking to the past in a search for a collective experience which might shed light on their present-day situation. Because of the breadth of issues raised by the current feminist movement, and because of our advantage of hindsight over the earlier movement, we have the opportunity to construct a women's history which will add greatly to our self-understanding. In addition, recent developments in historical writing, especially in the area of social history, make available to us new tools for the exploration of women's past.

The first generation of feminists in the nineteenth century began this inquiry and contributed a body of literature complementary to their own understanding of women's condition. The "Declaration of Sentiments" adopted at the 1848 Seneca Falls meeting claimed that the "history of mankind is a history of repeated injuries and usurpations on the part of man toward woman, having in direct object the establishment of an absolute tyranny over her." This approach, which set the theme for later decades of feminist writing, focused

1

on oppression as women's historical reality. Often these writers studied exceptional women who managed to overstep their prescribed roles, or they documented the momentous rise of the woman's movement. But these events were always cast against the obstacles restricting women's advancement. Basically, the early feminist historians created a chronology and analysis of women's age-old subjection to men.

This feminist interpretation of history was challenged by Mary Beard in <u>Woman</u> <u>as</u> <u>Force</u> <u>in</u> <u>History</u>, published in 1946. (1) Principally she questioned the emphasis on an endless history of subjection. That stress, she argued, prevented women from understanding the power they had held historically in all areas of social activity. Women had internalized the myth of their secondary status and enshrined it in an inadequate feminist analysis. Beard claimed that a study of domestic life and familial power would reveal a rich history of women's participation. Moreover, a genuine understanding of this participation in relation to the traditional concepts of economic, social, and political development would reframe the whole picture of history. To Mary Beard, this was not simply a "woman question" but a necessary prerequisite for "the realization of the noblest ideals in the history of humanity." (p. 340)

Mary Beard wrote in the shadow of World War II. After the defeat of fascism, women, she believed, would cast off their chains and emerge as leaders of world democracy. She accepted the inevitability of progress and envisioned women as the civilizing force of human history. Without accepting her faith, we believe it is important to recognize and respond to her insistence that women's history must not negate women's past. Mary Beard rightly believed that the true history of women's lives would be more important than a documentation of society's restrictions on their activities.

Faced again with the task of defining women's history, we find it essential to create a solid theoretical foundation. While lacking a faith in the saving powers of industrialism or of political democracy, we need to go well beyond the work of the early feminist historians. Any notion that the inner logic of "woman's sphere" is too slight to examine, and too slight to have had a significant effect on the course of history, has to be rejected.

That women have not had access to the means of social definition and have not lived and worked in the spheres of reward and recognition is obvious. They have lived in what Simone de Beauvoir has described as the historical anomaly of "the Other." But the problem remains: As objects, do we have a history, properly speaking? The seeming timelessness of women's lives may describe one source of the lack of female consciousness through long periods: the processes affecting their lives are frequently slow and without immediate impact on their awareness. But to assume that their lives were without time and without change, ignores the role that the subjection of women has played in world development. Historians' chronic blindness to that fact prevents them from probing the fullest meaning of history. If we can succeed in defining the "specificity of their oppression" (2), we will as well have moved closer to realizing the dynamics of all historical development — a necessary prerequisite for changing it.

The world women have inhabited has its own history, ultimately related on one hand to the changes in their lives, and on the other to the progress of world history, encompassing the lives of all people. The organization of society around age, the privatization of the family, and the emergence of a culture of motherhood around the biological function are instances of women's sphere being subject to historical analysis. As Philippe Aries demonstrated in Centuries of Childhood, the history of that intimate world is at the root of the changes in all modern social relations. (3) The disintegration of pre-industrial family relations mediated the transformation of all personal relations in response to changes of the means of production and the new stratification of social classes.

Historians and feminists alike have assumed that "woman" is a transhistorical creature who for purposes of discussion can be isolated from social development. Recently, some writers for the women's liberation movement have appropriated this concept, designating all other class, race, and historical conditions of women as secondary and derivative. For these writers, sex becomes the primary contradiction of life, and the male/female antagonism or dichotomy is designated as the theoretical principle underlying all history. In all present and past forms of society, according to this view, woman have constituted a distinct caste, linked together by their subordinate position in male-dominated culture. Caste, then, defines the negativity of women's relationships within the larger society. At the same time, this view sees the caste situation as holding the inherent seed of liberation. The oppressive isolation from male culture, which defines caste, somehow produces a powerful shared consciousness.

This notion of caste has two major shortcomings. First of all, an essentially static concept of oppression does not account for the changing degree to which women have consciously shared a collective identity. Thus, Simone de Beauvoir, who made a decisive contribution in defining the usefulness of what women have shared,

3

specifically rejected the idea that women have been a caste, because they have not reached a required consciousness of self. (4) Our history in fact must record the movement of women toward that consciousness and not assume that caste relationships necessarily make it inevitable. The second problem is that, in describing the bond between women in any particular period or across centuries, caste fails because it ignores the forms that oppression took at different times for different women. Women have been kept apart in their oppression, separated from one another. To assert centuries of sisterhood will not explain — or help overcome — the historic reality of antagonisms and conflicting experience. It is precisely the interrelationship between women's oppression and the "rest" of history that enables us to understand why, for example, black and white women in the ante-bellum South could not unite around their "common" oppression.

A paradoxical view of woman's proper role in society has developed out of the caste idea of women's historical condition. On one hand, women were said to have been denied the feeling of strength and the possession of real power which defined men's control over the world. On the other hand, by virtue of powerlessness women were assumed to have retained a kind of moral superiority over

THE BURDEN LONG AGO CALLED "WOMAN'S DUTY."

aggressive, warlike men. Women's suffrage advocates, for example, often claimed that women's moral values, preserved in the isolation of their own sphere, could lead to the uplifting of all humanity. Women, according to this view, will mend the world because their hands are clean from the blood, profit, and power with which men have ruled the world. This argument not only accepts a view of the past in which women were outside of history, but also asserts that now, and in the future, that condition which has separated them from men will be the basis for their entrance into history.

The bond women have always shared, in the caste argument, is their oppression. That women have suffered oppression is not to be denied. Sexual exploitation, ego damage, the double standard, stereotyping, and discrimination are past as well as present realities. But oppression has meant different things at different times to different groups and classes of women. For example, women today explain sexual exploitation partially in terms of the repressive nature of monogamy that binds a woman to one man. While men utilize women for their own gratification, they deny women the right to sexual fulfillment by specifying the forms of sexual activity. Many of the special complaints center on the denial to women of equal pleasure. Nineteenth Century feminists, on the other hand, accepted the Victorian double standard. For them, sexual exploitation referred most often to the necessity of vile sex to satisfy their vulgar, sensual husbands. Without effective birth control, liberation in practice meant chastity rather than free love. The forceful reaction of feminists against Victoria Woodhull's association with their movement reflected this tension.

The conceptual confusion created by the unvarying and undifferentiated term "oppression" can also be illustrated if we apply the same word to the condition of the white plantation mistress and the black slave woman. For the slave woman, oppression included physical cruelty and sexual exploitation; for the Southern Lady, oppression meant social and legal constrictions of another order. A single concept of oppression does little to explain the dynamic of either woman's life or the historical conditions underlying it. In addition, to ignore the important differences which distinguish the lives of the two women is to do violence to the history of black men and women under slavery.

The middle-class base of nineteenth-century feminism is frequently noted, lamented, and rejected as a model for today's movement. To transcend that limitation we must know as much about what kept women apart as we know about what brought them together. For example, working women in the last century often expressed their feelings in class terms and organized around their work. Women in ethnic communities recognized the hardships they shared with men of the same nationalities more often than they identified a common bondage with upper class or WASP women. Economic well-being, social relations, life expectancy, ranges of personal choice are dependent on the changing relations among classes in American society, and those conditions of daily life have been as real for women as for men.

With a caste analysis, then, the diversity in women's experience is underplayed, and as victims of oppression, women are assigned a static role rather than one allowing for change. In essence, history becomes an external process, a force which presses against women without a reciprocal interaction. Women become in the truest sense the objects of history, bound by their peculiar situation. The very real powerlessness felt and frequently expressed by women of the last two centuries becomes, ironically, a source of misunderstanding about the complexity of women's part in the history of humanity. Such generalization serves to mystify the real sources of women's power.

Without denying what we share as women, we must develop a framework that transcends the limitation of caste. As an element in history, oppression must be clearly recognized and overcome. But that still does not make oppression a truth which stands above all other historical and philosophical observations.

◘◘◘

Historians' neglect of women has derived from their ideas about historical significance. Their categories and periodization have been masculine by definition, for they have centered on public activity in the world of political and economic affairs. Traditionally, wars and politics have always been a part of "history," while those institutions which have affected individuals most immediately — social relationships, marriage, the family — have been outside "history." Men, given the traditional definition of historical significance, have been active; women, passive. Then too, historians are accustomed to measuring change by tangible and discrete events: wars are declared, a presidential administration begins and ends. By comparison, women's lives throughout western history are characterized by an apparent timelessness: their lives have focused on bearing and raising children and have been isolated within the confines of the family. The processes affecting women's lives frequently have been slow and without immediate impact. Too often, historians have assumed that women's lives were simply without time and without change. They thus ignore some very real developments and changes over history, and neglect the role the subjection of women has played in world development.

Even when historians have written directly on women in history, these assumptions have often crippled their writing. Women who look to the current body of historiography in order to gain a better understanding of the social forces which have shaped their lives will find that writing on women falls into four categories : 1) institutional histories of women in organizations, 2) biographies of important women, 3) histories of ideas about women and their roles,

ART SUPPLEMENT MILWAUKEE FREE PRESS          DESIGN FOR A BACHELOR'S WALL PAPER.          Drawn by CHARLES DANA GIBSON
Milwaukee, Wis., December 2, 1906                                                              Copyright, 1902, by Life Publishing Co.

and 4) social histories of women in particular times and places. The most exciting changes in recent years have occurred in the last category, as attitudes and methods new to historical inquiry have converged with questions new to feminism. The other modes persist, however, and their assumptions continue to influence our conceptions of women's past.

Histories of women in organizations make up the largest number of works on women. These institutional studies are more precisely labeled as histories of feminism rather than histories of women, for most of them are about women's-rights movements. Actually, the scope is even narrower, since they focus almost exclusively on the campaign for women's suffrage, to the neglect of other aspects of the woman movement. One is led to assume, through such studies as Eleanor Flexner's <u>Century of Struggle</u> and Mildred Adams'

The Right To Be People, that American feminism — or even women's history generally — is virtually synonymous with the fight for the vote. (5) In these studies, women's history begins in 1848, with the Seneca Falls Convention, and ends abruptly in 1920, with the ratification of the woman suffrage amendment. The subjects of institutional histories are women who were articulate, conscious members of organizations.

Although the abundance of source material on the women's-rights movement helps explain why historians have devoted so much attention to it, this fact alone does not fully explain why scholars have paid so little attention to women who were not involved in organized feminism. A more important explanation is most historians' assumption that only when women are behaving in ways usually regarded as masculine — that is, politically and collectively — do they merit historical discussion. In all other matters, many writers seem to dismiss women's experience as "women's work" — an inappropriate or irrelevant subject for historians who have always dealt with power relations and institutions. Thus, writers of institutional studies assume that women have had a history, properly speaking, only when they have managed to step out of their prescribed sphere and enter the world of men.

Secondly, many institutional studies share the assumption that organizations initiate social change in and of themselves. Too often there is no serious attempt to weigh the impact of industrialization, urbanization, and other socio-economic changes on the development of women's organizations. The early studies of the suffrage movement, such as Susan Anthony's, Elizabeth Cady Stanton's and Mathilda Gage's mammoth compendium The History of the Woman Suffrage Movement and Carrie Chapman Catt's Woman Suffrage and Politics, seem unaware of the changes that the nineteenth century brought to women's lives. (6) Even many of their more recent counterparts seem to be written in the same kind of historical vacuum.

Finally, the writers who have dealt extensively with women's rights and suffrage movements have generally shared a faith in American political democracy and a belief in the linear progression of American history. For most of them, women's history is set in an evolutionary framework depicting the development of western civilization as the unfolding progress of humanity toward democracy. In this conception, the woman movement can be interpreted as "another chapter in the struggle for liberty." (7) Although most recent studies have been more sophisticated in writing and research than the studies of suffrage workers themselves, they have often shared the optimistic Progressive notion of historical development. Mildred Adams, for example, writes in The Right to be People:

> It was a remarkably selfless campaign. The women who spent their lives in it were working not for themselves, but for the common good. They were working for the better status of women in a democracy and for the better conduct of that democracy. They honestly believed that women ... should have the vote because they were citizens and as a tool with which to improve not only their own legal status, but also the laws and government of the nation. (8)

This Progressive viewpoint, largely unconscious in the early writers who chronicled the progress of their own movement with optimism and sincerity, obscures many important facets of the women's-rights movement, not to mention women's history in general. Women enlisted in the suffrage movement for a variety of reasons. A women's-club member, for example, had different reasons for working for suffrage than a young industrial worker. Progressive interpretations have usually neglected the racist aspect of the early suffrage movement, its limited middle-class concerns, and its lack of feminist ideology.

Aileen Kraditor's The Ideas of the Woman Suffrage Movement, William O'Neill's Everyone Was Brave: The Rise and Fall of Feminism in America, and William Chafe's The American Woman: Her Changing Social, Economic, and Political Roles, 1920–1970 serve in some ways as correctives to older studies. (9) Kraditor traces the development of the suffragists' ideology from nineteenth-century arguments based on natural rights to the arguments based on the need for women's participation in social and political reform in the early twentieth century. Her work illuminates the suffragists' abandonment of far-reaching feminist reform in favor of an expedient rationale for voting rights based on traditional notions of femininity. In addition, her study sheds light on the suffragists' class base. She emphasizes the middle-class nature of the movement and its basic failure, despite assertions of "sisterhood," to overcome the limits of class interests and outlook.

William O'Neill, in Everyone Was Brave and in his article, "Feminism as a Radical Ideology" (10), also emphasizes the suffrage movement's middle-class base and the suffragists' failure to formulate a radical critique of the existing social structure. He documents the process by which American feminists discarded potentially radical ideas about marriage and the family and replaced them with the goals of "social feminism" geared toward general social reform.

William Chafe's study  The American Woman  departs from traditional institutional studies by analyzing women's historical experience in the years after the suffrage amendment was passed. Chafe applies sociological role theory and the anthropological concept of the divison of labor by sex to his analysis. He argues that the suffrage amendment failed to alter woman's role in any fundamental way because it offered a political solution to a social problem. Changes in women's legal, political, and economic history from 1920 to 1940 were a consequence of changing employment patterns more than of winning the vote.

All three historians, however, despite their greater sophistication in analyzing the woman movement and its ideological limitations, are still confined by the traditional emphasis on women's public lives. The content of women's everyday experiences and the

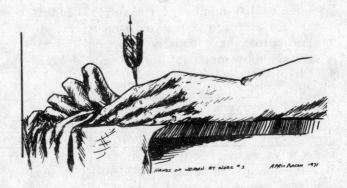

HANDS OF WOMAN AT WORK #3      APRIL RACON 1971

relationships between their public and private lives remain hidden. Even the best of the strictly institutional studies, then, are inherently limited in the scope of their inquiry.

Histories of the women's-rights movement and of women's organizations are important, and, despite the numerous studies already published on the early movement, many questions remain unanswered. New questions need to be asked, drawn from our experience in the present movement. For example, why did the first feminist movement ultimately lose sight of feminist goals? What can we learn from the early women's-rights movements' tactics? What can we learn about the nature and development of feminist consciousness? We also have a great deal to learn from studies of other types of women's organizations, when we break away from historians' overwhelming emphasis on women's suffrage. The women's-club movement, the temperance crusade, women's participation in labor unions, and the special role women played in early twentieth-century social-reform organizations and the settlement movements are just being written about or have yet to be explored.

Biography, the second major form of historical writing on women, has often served as the only way to reconstruct the lives women lead. Sources which exist for writing about the world of men do not exist for the majority of women during most periods of history. Biographies can tell us very little, however, about the life style of the overwhelming majority of women who were not members of a small social elite or who did not pioneer in one of the professions. The work of reconstructing the history of the inarticulate has just begun, and women make up the largest and probably the most silent of society's inarticulate groups. Anyone who has attempted genealogical and demographic research knows that even basic facts about the birth, death, and parenthood of a woman in most historical periods are difficult to find.

Few women have left diaries, letters, or other written sources with which to assess their role and their experience. The very existence of written materials on a woman tells us that she was exceptional : she had the leisure and ability to write, she had the opportunity to experience something other than basic production for her household, and she lived in a family conscious enough of its heritage to preserve family records. Sometimes the existence of written sources on a woman indicates only that she was married to a famous man. Alice Desmond's biography, <u>Alexander</u> <u>Hamilton's</u> <u>Wife</u> (1954), is a good case in point. Even when written sources exist, they often prove sadly inadequate to the task of reconstructing a meaningful narrative of a woman's life. The lack of feminist consciousness characteristic of a pre-industrial society made it highly unusual for a woman to write of herself in letters or diaries in a self-conscious way, distinguishing her experience from the experiences of her husband and children. Thus, biography is most useful in understanding the exceptional woman who stands out in history, such as Anne Hutchinson, the Grimke sisters, Margaret Sanger, or Emma Goldman. Uncovering the experiences of "typical" women, or even defining what "typical" means, however, is far more difficult.

Most biographies are limited also because they are narrative and anecdotal : writers often emphasize a subject's unique or eccentric traits at the expense of analyzing how the subject fit into her social environment. A woman's uniqueness is exaggerated because the biographer does not know the options and expectations his subject had, nor does he have perspective on the time, place, and conditions in which she lived and worked. In essence, then, the woman is removed from history.

The psychological assumptions with which biographers have approached their subjects have also affected their work. Writers have worked, often unconsciously, within the confines of psychological theories of woman's nature. Freudian constructs have been the basis for most of their conceptualizations. American historians, in the tradition of psychoanalytic theory, have generally assumed that woman is a naturally passive creature. Although recent debate over the validity of psychoanalytic constructs has made historians more cautious about broad generalizations, Freud's ideas retain a vogue at a popular level, providing norms for judging deviance. The recurring statement that Mary Wollstonecraft, or any other feminist, refused her passive social role because of an extreme case of penis envy is the most obvious example of a loose application of a Freudian model to women's history. Similarly, we sometimes read that women who rejected their prescribed roles did so because of unresolved Oedipal conflicts or fixations at immature developmental stages. (11)

Recent psychological theories have recognized that individuals can formulate and adhere to ideologies as the result of rational observation of their environment's need for change rather than as an attempt to work out unconscious inner conflicts. Margaret George's biography of Mary Wollstonecraft, One Woman's Situation, is an excellent example of a study which does not confound the subject's personal psychological make-up with her feminist politics. For the most part, however, biographers have employed psychological theories in an unsophisticated, piecemeal, and reductionistic manner, failing to realize that psychological theories cannot, and are not intended to, explain the totality of historical experience.

The third form of women's history, the history of social ideas, poses a question common to all historical writing: what is the relationship between ideas and social practice? Histories of social ideas are often based on prescriptive literature such as etiquette books, child-rearing and marriage manuals, and home-economics texts — literature, in other words, written to inform contemporaries how they ought to conduct their lives.

These prescriptive studies ask important questions about the nature of social institutions. They attempt to chart changes and developments in childrearing practices, marriage and divorce customs, and sexual mores, and to relate those developments to a larger ideological framework. Edmund Morgan in The Puritan Family, for example, used sermons and Puritan writings to relate seventeenth-century Puritan theology to New England family life. Bernard Wishy, in The Child and the Republic, placed changes in attitudes toward children within a context of changing conceptions of environment as a determinant of a child's character. (12)

Although such studies ask important questions, they are often weak in the evidence they employ to answer them. After reading such works, we are left with vague and sometimes inaccurate notions about the nature of actual cultural behavior. We cannot assume that the models of behavior and attitudes found in sermons, books, or magazines accurately reflected how people really acted. Was a Puritan minister describing how his congregation behaved when he wrote about childrearing or woman's role, or was he describing ideals for his congregation to emulate? Did articles in Godey's Ladies' Book and other women's magazines describe how middle-class and upper-class parents actually treated their children? Prescriptive studies assume a relationship between ideology and social practice which may not always exist.

Histories of social ideas also fail to distinguish between women of different classes. Even if we take the largest estimate of Godey's circulation, an estimate which assumes that women handed one issue around among themselves, the majority of American families never saw a copy. To say "the child" or "the mother" on the basis of such literary and class-oriented work greatly oversimplifies the complexity of behavior and the class differences in social practice. Finally, too little attention is given to social and economic factors in the histories of social ideas by concentrating on the words of a few taste setters.

The fourth category of studies in women's history, which we have given the general label of social history, holds the greatest possibilities for future work. New advances in historical methodology coupled with feminist questions promise to expand our knowledge of women's lives throughout American history.

Social histories of women are not new. In the early years of the twentieth century, when a feminist movement was strong, a number of women wrote of their past with historical skill and feminist consciousness. Although oversimplified by today's standards of social history, books such as Julia Spruill's Women's Life and Work in the Southern Colonies, Elisabeth Dexter's Colonial Women of Affairs, and Edith Abbott's Women in Industry (13) still stand out as exemplary efforts to describe the tasks that women performed, the resources they had, the values they held, and the self-assertion they exhibited. Each book required painstaking surveys of sources which had only peripheral bearing on family life to discover hints of women's activities. The best of the social histories distinguished between women in cities and in rural areas, between planters' wives and female slaves, between immigrants and WASPs. They took account of changes over time, as in Elizabeth Dexter's careful tracing of the contractions in women's opportunities in the late eighteenth and early nineteenth centuries.

Recent social histories of women in America have also stressed the ways women's roles and sphere have changed over time. For example, historians have begun to look at the relationship of women's movements to major social changes in American society rather than as isolated groups of atypical and eccentric women. Social changes in mid-nineteenth-century America affected woman's role in the family, the work that she performed, and ideas about femininity. Although we still do not have precise notions about how burgeoning industrialization affected women, we are beginning to look for connections between social change and the emergence of the nineteenth-century women's-rights movement. (14)

The new social history has begun to affect the way that biographers treat their subjects. A number of recent books have depicted prominent women in relation to their social environment rather than removing them from history and elevating them into heroines. Without denying that women such as Sarah and Angelina Grimke, Mary Wollstonecraft, and Margaret Sanger were exceptional individuals, recent biographies of these women have placed them squarely within the historical context of their lives. Gerda Lerner in her biography The Grimke Sisters From South Carolina deals with Angelina and Sarah Grimke as women who grew up in the American antebellum South, in a Quaker family, and analyzes the content and development of their feminism and abolitionism from this frame of reference. Margaret George discusses Mary Wollstonecraft in One Woman's Situation as an archetypal example of the eighteenth-century bourgeois woman, delineates the options open to a woman of her class, and analyzes Wollstonecraft's feminism as a product of both her personal life and her historical situation. David Kennedy, in Birth Control in America: The Career of Margaret Sanger, traces Sanger's career within the context of attitudes toward sexuality and medical developments in contraception. All three studies serve as examples of sympathetic analyses which attempt to integrate personal motivational factors and the external social environment. (15)

Social historians are also beginning to probe the connections between woman's role in the home and the work she has performed in the labor force. We are becoming aware that we cannot separate the two roles. Because different class and ethnic groups within American society have had varying family structures and cultural mores regarding woman's role, industrialization did not affect all women in the same ways. Virginia McLaughlin's study of Italian immigrant family patterns in Buffalo, New York is an excellent example of new ways of examining the impact of social change on

C. BURNETT '44

women. Her study illustrates the strength and adaptability of traditional pre-industrial family patterns in an industrial society. In addition, her study is important for pointing out the necessity for separate analyses of women's experiences in different classes and ethnic groups. (16)

Finally, historians are delving more deeply into women's awareness of social change and their ways of dealing with it. We are trying to understand how women resisted or tried to circumvent the restrictions placed upon them and how they came to terms with their societal role. In other words, feminist historians are asking what it was like to be a woman at various times in history. At present most of these studies are biographical essays of nineteenth-century women writers who revealed their feelings about womanhood through the medium of fiction. For example, Tillie Olsen's biographical essay on Rebecca Harding Davis combines literary analysis of Harding's writings with an insightful discussion of how Harding's fictional characters expressed her own sense of frustration at being confined to a life of "'unused powers, thwarted energies, starved hopes.'" (17) But historians are also starting to look at other activities besides writing as avenues of women's self-expression. Some of the new studies of women in organizations, while not neglecting the organizational activities themselves, have tried to explore what needs women were fulfilling by participating in moral-reform societies, religious movements, and settlement houses. (18) The history of organized feminism, if undertaken from this viewpoint, would have much to tell us about the process by which women began to think of themselves as women, with distinct status and distinct problems. Beyond that, we also need to know much more about working-class women's subjective responses to industrialization and unionization, and how a woman worker's responses to life in the work place were affected by her perceptions of her role as a woman.

In short, new approaches to women's history are attempting to integrate women into the mainstream of American historical development rather than isolating women as a separate category. Although most new social histories could still be classified in institutional, biographical, or prescriptive categories, more historians are placing their work in a larger historical and social context.

Perhaps, as recent work suggests, we are now at a turning point in the nature of the researches. At last, some categories have been established for a social history which seeks the story of women not only as such, but also within the general historical developments that have shaped human action and understanding. We are learning that the writing of women into history necessarily involves redefining and enlarging traditional notions of historical significance, to encompass personal, subjective experience as well as public and political activities. It is not too much to suggest that, however hesitant the actual beginnings, such a methodology implies not only a new history of women, but also a new history.

PART II

The changes which took place in the lives of women during the colonial period — a span of almost two centuries — provide a valuable framework for an understanding of the relationship between greater economic and social complexity and the emergence of a distinct, and limiting, notion of femininity. At one end of the period there was the Virginia House of Burgesses describing why it granted land to wives as well as to husbands in 1619: " ... in a new plantation it is not knowen (sic) whether man or woman be the most necessary." (19) At the other there was Mercy Otis Warren (1728-1814), a writer and historian, writing to a young woman that learning was useless to a lady (as useless as virtue to a gentleman). (20)

In this discussion we can point out some of the general outlines of colonial growth and some of the signs that transformations were occurring in daily life. At a minimum, the suggestions here should provide background for the more familiar tale of the Nineteenth Century, when the proscriptions on women and the definitions of their limited sphere were fully developed.

Colonial history was in part a beginning again. Each new coastal settlement and each move westward entailed a return to the simplest social organization: A family or a single man produced enough for survival and used virtually all available time for essential work. There were numerous sequences of development in different locations, and while one city may have resembled an English city, farms on the frontier were no doubt more similar to the earliest settlements. Still no one moved for long beyond the influence of colonial governments, and in most areas churches were established as rapidly as settlers moved in.

Colonial forms of increasing complexity, models for institutions and for social relations, came out of the European (primarily English) experience of the settlers. The majority of colonists, for example, accepted the logic of monogamous marriage, built single family houses, and assumed their right to own property. (21) They became members of churches with British or European counterparts, adopted elements of English common law, and organized their production and marketing along familiar lines. By the middle of the Eighteenth Century, when commerce, or reliance on commerce, created not only greater involvement with the mother country but greater similarities with it as well, colonists increasingly sought to duplicate the forms of English social life. (22)

Women throughout the period were tied to the fate of the family. Towns in New England assumed and legislated a family basis for social life, and single women were urged to live within a family household. (23) In some of the Southern colonies where settlement was initially conducted as an adventure by English investors, men were sent alone to begin productive work. It was found that little incentive for producing a surplus existed without families, so women were imported and sold to men for the cost of their passages. (24) That brief period may express as much about the importance of women in colonial development as any time when they were more conspicuous by their presence. Throughout the colonies the sex ratio between men and women favored women — a development unique to American society. As a result a woman's chance of marrying, her economic support, was very high and the age at which she married was significantly lower than in England. It may have been true, as well, that the scarcity of women resulted in greater social mobility for women; they were in such demand that they could afford to choose. (25)

Purchase brides for the Adventurers in Virginia, about 1621. (From the Collections of the Library of Congress)

The simplicity of economic and social organization concentrated a variety of essential activities in the family. In family production each member contributed work of equal importance to the group's survival. Two aspects of this were no doubt important in providing women with useful roles: the independence of each family's work and the immediate necessity of it. The division of work was mostly along sex lines, but within that basic division of labor there were different patterns, depending on the relative wealth of the family, the degree of participation in a cash economy, the organization of the husband's work, and the size of the household — relatives, servants or slaves, numbers of children, et cetera. Most families were farming, producing their own food, some surplus for trade, and their own clothing, soap, candles, and fuel. In this setting a large family was an asset, and thus the reproductive role of the mother, as well as her productive work, was valued. (26)

Education for the majority of colonists was something that took place in the family and consisted of teaching skills and morals. Boys and girls learned those from the work and daily life of their families. Where families were concentrated and homogeneous, as in New England towns or religious settlements, children occasionally attended schools or were traded into another family to learn skills or manners. (27) Mrs. Anna Grant, resident in New York before the Revolution, recorded in her Memoirs that among the Dutch in Albany, mothers took primary responsibility for educating children, especially for religious teaching. Janet Schaw, an Eighteenth Century traveler in North Carolina, noted that the sharp contrast in civility between men and women was a result of daughters being raised in the cultured environment of their homes while sons learned the rough and fighting ways of the woods from their fathers. Whatever its particular form, this responsibility to society, resting with the family, defined a major part of the work of both mothers and fathers. Not until education was more clearly defined as something that changed the relationship between parents and children by introducing new values into a society, and until the family unit was no longer concentrated with the work of both men and women, did learning require new structures and distinct duties of each parent. (28)

The accompanying rhetoric about marriage described a partnership between man and woman. The institution existed to produce offspring and, at least in Puritan thought, to control the natural sexual appetites by providing an outlet for their monogamous expression. In New England grounds for divorce applied equally to each sex: adultery, impotency, refusal of sexual favors, and desertion. However the Puritans, so often chided for their repressive attitudes toward sex, delimited only two major forms of deviation: Sexuality must never interfere with the ultimate relationship, that between human and God; and it must never take place outside of marriage. In practice, those restrictions may in fact have loosened during the Eighteenth Century, as records of children born to couples after less than nine months of marriage indicate. Other colonies appear to have accepted a double standard of sexual behavior somewhat earlier, at least in the application of the law. The partnership had economic reality when the family worked the land or in a craft and so long as the wealth provided for children derived from that common work. (29)

Throughout most of the Seventeenth Century, colonial society was relatively unfragmented, either by sex or by age. (30) Individual women occasionally stepped outside the limits set for them (Anne Hutchinson's doctrinal challenge to Massachusetts leaders, Quaker missionaries asserting the necessity of religious tolerance, a Southern woman refusing to utter the word "obey" in her marriage vow); but in general, neither men nor women seemed concerned with defining what women were or what their unique contribution to society should be. (31) Similarly, studies of children's toys, books, and care reveal very little special attention to children's particularity in the society. (32) The cultural expressions of the time indicate lack of consciousness about the possible differences which later came to characterize all discussion of women and children.

The emphasis on the social necessity of women in a wilderness environment and the consequent respect given to their labor must not be mistaken for a society without discriminations against women. Distinctions were made in laws, in education, in theology and church affairs, and in political and property rights. No one asserted equality. But there was flexibility in drawing the lines around women's work and men's work. Abstract theories about the proper role of women did not stand in the way of meeting familial and social needs. There is considerable evidence that women were engaged in numerous business and professional activities in the colonial period. Their work was not simply in those jobs extending their traditional domestic work out into more complex organization, such as production of foodstuffs and clothing. Women published and printed newspapers, managed tanneries, kept taverns, and engaged in just about every occupation existing in the colonies. Many of these women, who had learned the skills of the trade while sharing the work of their husbands, were working as widows to support their families. (33)

This "unique" presence of women is frequently taken to be a sign of the liberating effect of frontier conditions on traditional roles; but this view ignores the work experience of English women. In England, women had been members of craft guilds, had worked in their husbands' jobs as widows, and had been accepted in such professional capacities as midwives and attorneys in lieu of their husbands. But by the end of the Seventeenth Century women had lost those positions. Comparison with the more carefully documented English events throws new light on the origins of the colonial freedom so often located. Nothing in English culture or production militated against utilizing the talents of men and women in a variety of occupations as long as the economy needed their strength and numbers. When that need ended, and when women found their access to jobs limited by law or by their inability to gain the prerequisites, their presence sharply declined. However, a series of transformations in the organization of work protected the opportunities for male work (in the dying craft guilds, for example) and at the same time excluded women by edict or default. Two activities in the colonies underwent this limiting process: midwifery and the informal exercise of power of attorney. (34)

Midwifery was not only open to women; their monopoly was protected. In 1675 officials of York County, Maine presented "Captain Francis Raine for presuming to act the part of a midwife", and fined him fifty shillings. (35) But less than a century later formal learning began to replace practical experience for the job. Doctor William Shippen Junior — a leader in medical education in Philadelphia — announced a series of lectures on midwifery in 1765. He did not exclude women from training, but offered his expertise to women with "virtue enough to own their ignorance". Not only was there a serious problem about mortality rates in childbirth, but the situation was aggravated "by the unskillful old women...." (36) A similar process in the granting of powers of attorney has been documented in Maryland. Law became a career with prerequisites denied to women, and gradually the practical flexibility which had allowed women to appear in court in their own behalf if single or in behalf of their husband in his absence was abandoned. (37)

Similarly, by the middle of the Eighteenth Century the manifestations of a distinct world for upper-class women with its own standards of success and necessities were clearly emerging in the colonies. The culture was in part imported from England, but rapidly developed parallel but indigenous forms. A frequently cited instance is the interest in women's education. Special schools were opened in the major coastal towns of Boston, Newport, New York, Philadelphia, and Charleston. After the Revolution, female seminaries extended further inland. (38) These schools were designed to prepare women for their roles as wives and mothers. Some academic subjects such as appeared in the schools for boys were selected as suitable, but primarily the schools concentrated on styles of ladylike qualities and skills. Some theorists of this new education particularly aimed at providing what Abigail Adams called the "groundwork...of more durable colors"; they wanted to teach women to respect the serious literature of philosophy and morality, to read history and thus to be better prepared to talk intelligently with their husbands and to introduce their children to the great works of civilization. Others were more concerned with needlework and table manners, with dancing and carriage. To attract a suitable husband, to be a credit to his success, and to keep a good house after marriage seemed the primary goal for educated girls.

Education as a means to expand experience and to enlarge the opportunities of an individual was not considered for this particular field of learning and teaching.

Benjamin Rush, the alleged truly American theorist of female education, brought home in his writing the new needs that the society had to meet. (39) In an agressive and competitive economic system some stability was needed next to each man to protect the wealth of the family; thus women needed training as stewards and guardians of their husbands' money. Without a docile servant class, American women needed special skills to manage their domestic work force. Fathers were no longer at home all the time, and the burdens of raising children fell particularly on women who had to recognize their new duty toward children and receive some training to perform the work. Education according to Rush and the other theorists would condition women to their limited sphere in the home.

Prior to the middle of the century the primary source of ideas to "define" woman in an objective way was in theology, where her secondary status was clearly established, but not without granting her equal access to the final and more important rewards in the hereafter. The change came first through imported and reprinted English essays, novels, and prescriptive books. Later educated colonial men (and, even later, colonial women) wrote their own contributions presenting their views on fashions, on what and how women thought, on the manners of courting these odd creatures and the doom of marrying one. Such manner of writing had developed earlier in England, particularly addressed to men, as the idea grew that gentility or whatever qualities were valued in society were not inherited but could be acquired. Men delighted in describing their ideal woman, an ideal which women were then expected to emulate. The Lady — stylish, learned within limits, inconspicuously managerial with her servants, and tolerant of masculine foibles — existed, in this literature, for a gentleman's pleasure and display. Everything about the feminine life turned around her ability to please her husband by standards that he established. Although it is unlikely that women lived out or up to this ideal, their self-conscious attention to an earthly, domestic ideal was assumed. The life of Nancy Shippen, an upper-class Philadelphia belle unhappily married by her father's wishes, reveals some of the practical pain of living through the literary images of female life. (40)

In the literary record the progress of femininity was not altogether smooth. Despite a few native articles, some individual reactions to the published descriptions of women and the tyrannical practice of men, and widespread knowledge of the ideas of Mary Wollstonecraft in her Vindication of the Rights of Women, no framework was established to integrate the individual responses. Women might use their learning for more than their domestic success and teach school or try to support themselves by writing, but those changes did not serve as a basis for challenging the essential limitations of women's lives. (41)

British "sentimental" novels were more widely read than vindications and feminist dialogues. They were tales of seduction and of battles for female virtue against lustful male tempters, in which sensibility and domestic love triumphed over the temptations of flesh and passion. (42) Samuel Richardson's Pamela won readers' hearts by her heroic struggles against her employer who was, as Pamela saw it, intent on seducing her. In a later American counterpart, The Coquette, the heroine tried to rebel against decorum but died ignominiously for her efforts. In each of these stories the essential human struggle was transferred from one with abstract evil to one between the sexes. And the first victim in that transformation was healthy sex.

The morality of sentimentalism, however, defined a series of almost religious tests faced only by women and met by successfully avoiding participation in a masculine world of physical and degrading passion. Not only was the course charted highly repressive of both men and women, but it also set the central conflict of life between the sexes. The success of this formula for the upper class continued well into the Nineteenth Century, but its rules and some of its best best-sellers made their appearance before the Revolution in the colonies.

꒱

By the end of the Eighteenth Century, the development of a market economy had begun to disrupt and transform the social relations of the family. Pre-industrial labor, as Marx noted, was based on a spontaneous or natural division of work within the family, depending on tradition and differences in age and sex to determine productive roles. The labor power of each individual member was only a "definite portion of the labor power of the family" expressed in products — whether crops, livestock, or clothing. By the first decades of the Nineteenth Century, the growth of manufacturing in home industries had already challenged the basis of these relations by widening the division of labor within the family, and by widening class divisions between families. The development of a true factory system was slow during this period: As late as 1810 two-thirds of the clothing and household textiles of persons living outside the cities was produced by family manufacture. Yet for women this shift was significant. As products formerly produced at home came to be accessible on the common market, whether textiles, (several) food products, or household supplies like soap and wax, the prestige of women's labor inevitably declined. Moreover, the increasing expression of products as commodities, defined not primarily by their use value but rather by their exchange value on the market, dichotomized those produced under market conditions by socially-organized labor (that is, almost entirely by men) and those produced privately for direct use (that is, substantially by women and children in the home). The consequent mystification of the exchange process within society was called by Marx commodity fetishism, for it apparently replaced the pre-industrial, direct relationship between producers with "material relationships between persons and social relationships between things." (43) In a society of commodities, the subordinate and secondary value of women's work and of women themselves was necessarily degraded. To replace the spontaneous and relatively egalitarian division of labor in pre-industrial society had come a mode of organization which far more than before thrust women into the role of caring for the home, while men engaged in activities to reshape the world. Furthermore women's participation in the market economy was mediated through their husbands, thus relegating their own class, status, or privilege to a social function of their husbands' work.

CUPID, AUCTIONEER.

Similarly, the development of industrial capitalism transformed the roles of the family. While previously the family structure had encompassed a variety of forms and functions, the Nineteenth Century family tended to contract into an increasingly privatized set of relations. The compartmentalization of work and home activities was accompanied by a re-evaluation of women (and especially leisured women) as the guardians of traditional moral values. Within rapid industrialization men were necessarily an increasing part of social changes while women were ironically sacrificed for the preservation of a home which had lost its functional role in the economy. The home became "woman's sphere", fixed in terms of an Ideal rather than a realistic evaluation of women's potential roles. The older traditions of feminine usefulness, strength, and duty were cast aside for moral and decorative functions, and subjugation to domesticity became the most revered feminine virtue. Men, on the other hand, commonly were expected to show the inevitable effects of materialistic and base associations of a business life: aggression, vulgarity, hardness, and rationality. (44)

From these new definitions of men and women flowed the reappraisal of the Lady. Earlier, certain colonial imitations of British writings on manners and morals prescribed the gentility, style, limited education, and tolerance that could be expected from women of fashion; and in the South, this Imperial practice was greatly emulated. But not until the late Eighteenth Century did the Lady become the paragon for all American women. Colonial women generally, by contrast, had been respected because of the strength and sensuality of their characters, attributes which complemented their participation in the rugged family arrangement of an agricultural and frontier economy. As late as 1890, nearly half of all American women lived and worked in this immediate social environment of a farm family, providing many necessities for the home through daily hard work. Yet the farm wife lost her cultural standing to a new sector of women: the wives and daughters of the rising entrepreneurs and merchant capitalists of the urban Northeast. This new sector remained a numerical minority, while its ethos became central to the American Woman's self-definition. Because of their class position, these women gained a hegemony over female cultural patterns never attained by the Eighteenth Century elites. Taste, customs, religious and political principles, and above all morality were reshaped in the Nineteenth Century through the cultural equivalent of the economic power that capitalists themselves wielded. Thus for all women in the society, this new ideal of femininity became the model, however unrealizable it might be in their own lives. (45)

The Nineteenth Century replacement for woman's earlier role in the family was in fact idleness, expressed positively as gentility. The cultural manifestation of this ideal has been aptly called "The Cult of True Womanhood", for the rigid standards held by society amounted to religious-like rites. The True Woman symbolized and actualized stability, expressed in her own cardinal virtues of piety, purity, submissiveness, and domesticity. Religious literature and feminine novels continued and broadened a chaste idealization begun in the Eighteenth Century, and the newer women's journals emphasized the superficial and fashionable glamor of woman's new image. The functional character of household life was in effect replaced with an ornamental attraction of the Fair Lady. Since industrial ethics defined work as masculine, labor of almost any kind was deemed unsuitable for this Lady. Even gardening, a family necessity and appropriate pastime for colonial women, was perceived as a violation of the dainty image. While some contemporary journalists approved of flower cultivation (itself an apparent reflection of Victorian femininity), the usual editorial position unqualifiedly condemned the sight of a virtuous women tending an onion patch. Thus woman was in a sense transformed from a human being into a living object of art, existing for the pleasure and pride of her husband. She was a creature of solely decorative worth, possessing a beauty which rested on her frailty, delicacy, purity, and even asexuality. Woman's aesthetic contribution was herself, with her sensuality sublimated in the same sense in which Freud suggested that all Art was sublimated sexuality. Feminine culture was a highly romanticized shell, containing an apparently barren interior. (46)

The new demands on woman were expressed in a subtle but significant language of repression, reflecting and reshaping the very conceptions of its users. During this period, for instance, the substitution of "limb" for leg or arm first appeared, to the point of ruthless false consciousness where a breast of chicken was renamed "light meat". Correct table manners forbade offering a lady the chicken's leg; rather, she always received the "bosom", a common euphemism for this part. In polite company women were referred to as "ladies" or "females", in deference to the risque connotations of the womb in the more familiar generic label. In the areas of children and family, linguistic repression demanded a sheer absence of some vital discussions. Woman's newer interest in child rearing and infant care was paralleled by an accompanying secrecy involving pregnancy. Despite the rich detail in women's magazines on children's clothing, stories, and habits, pregnancy itself was proscribed even in the intimate relations of mother and daughter. Gestation was hidden as long as possible and then obscured by the retiring of the prospective mother into confinement. At last, even the term "pregnant" was replaced with the more delicate indirect suggestions like "with child" or "woman's condition". Such conditions viewed as mysterious and wonderful beyond contemplation involved a new level of Victorian myth making, such as the strange appearance of the stork. (47)

THE SPAHI:

Spring wrap, made of very rich black silk and trimmed with a deep twisted chenille fringe. The bonnet is composed of black Neapolitan and white silk figured with chenille.

New cultural restrictions in Victorian fashion dictated the spread of sexual repressiveness to all aspects of social life. Feminine passivity was ensured by clothing which, through the sheer weight and number of garments, literally enclosed women from the outside world and severely limited their physical mobility. The home was transformed from functionalism to the atmosphere of the showplace, an apt surrounding for the Victorian woman. Similarly, cleanliness standards of domestic life matched the purity associated with such a feminine setting. More subtle circumscriptions were easily noticed by European travelers such as Harriet Martineau, who, in her accounts of American society, frequently remarked on the relative severity of woman's domestic subjugation. Martineau implied that the discrepancy between the self-proclaimed democratic ideals of the Republic and the actual condition of American life was best exemplified in the treatment of women. Her books, which pointed to romantic chivalry as sheer substitution for real freedom were not considered proper reading materials for American ladies. With Mary Wollstonecraft and other rebels, she was vilified as a half-woman or mental hermaphrodite. (48)

Nineteenth Century repressive sexuality was in fact only one manifestation of the total work ethic that required suppression of all social values previously associated with leisure and enjoyment. While the appearance of new wealth nominally provided new free time, the ascending capitalist norms demanded an individual sacrifice to work, especially among male members of the rising entrepreneurial classes. The accompanying social relationships altered the fundamental conditions of life for man and woman, based substantially on a sexual polarity established through the industrial revolution. This polarity took various forms of expression. While sex came to be considered dirty, base, and vile, gratification became part of masculine culture, based on the materialistic functions of male social life. Woman's superior nature depended on the absence of painful and humiliating sexual participation, save for the satisfaction of her husband and the propagation of the race. Since the relationship between husband and wife was considered based on property, the male could easily acquire added property without seriously affecting his current holdings. Consequently, promiscuity was allowed only for men, who thereby participated in the rise of prostitution. (49)

Evidence of the effectiveness of female repression may be ascertained in the decline of the birth rate from 1820 to the end of the century. For a society lacking in knowledge of contraceptive measures, such decline could only signify the moderation of sexual relations for the prescribed bearers of society's children. Simultaneously the increasing urbanization and privatization of life had enhanced the importance of family individual members. The new status within the family tended to derive from individual worth rather than from group function. Thus while the existence of many children imposed a financial hardship upon the father's income, the single child became more precious and idealized. Childhood was extended to nearly marriageable age, since the presence of few children lowered the burden of dependency. Repression thereby was provided with a new outlet, if not a resolution, through the intensified relationship of mother and child. (50)

The double standard ironically intensified the sexual connotations of all social roles. Critics of Victorian society complained of an "over sexed" concern for life, referring not to the presence of uncontrollable urges but rather to the overly obsessive consciousness of the gender of the individual. European travelers often noted the inhibiting effects of the separation of men and women in all public affairs and attributed the low level of American intellectual culture to the stifling effect of women's segregation. Yet isolation both allowed and forced an advanced sector to search out a special identity, to comprehend and finally act on it. The very nature of Victorian society encouraged women to regard themselves as a special group, as <u>womanhood</u>. (51)

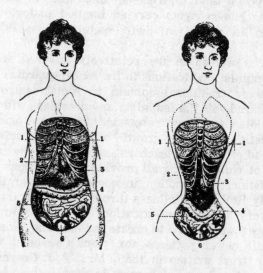

*Above: Effects of lacing on the female body. (1-lungs, 2-liver, 3-stomach, 4-great-gut, 5-small intestine, 6-bladder).*

The assertion of woman's moral superiority had some important implications. For the first time, women as a group had been attributed an independent power of moral guardianship that, however intellectually degrading, contained the potential of a hidden challenge to woman's traditional political and social passivity. In community reforms, such as sewing and literary circles, middle-class women recognized the advantages in their forced isolation. Through closer contact with each other, these women gained a new sense of sorority for their common plight and their common aspirations. (52)

These early organizational forms provided models for the later women's rights movement. Political consciousness was added through women's participation in the major reform movements of the times, most of all Temperance and Abolitionism. Women gained organizational skills and a recognition that leadership was not an exclusively male capacity. By the end of the 1840s, many activists realized that they would not be satisfied with shaping the world indirectly through their moral influence, and demanded the right to personal liberty and control of their own property. The debates on slavery attended by women especially sharpened their awareness, since many of the issues posed concerning basic human rights carried implied analogies to women's deprivation and its basis in their material possession by white men. (53)

Most American women in the relatively leisured middle classes rejected the Feminist implications in the moral-guardian theory which would extend their traditional domain to social controversy. While these women shared with the feminists an uneasiness with the ideals of gentility and idleness, they responded to a new functionalism of woman's domestic role. The growth of "domestic science" for the home, the spread of women's teachers' schools, and the rationalization of new modes of child-rearing all provided reassertions in new forms of woman's distinct contribution to society. However the attempt to shore up family life and wifeliness through further training inevitably undercut the very aim of domestication, for a few women exposed to outside influences were bound to create, as did Jane Addams and other reformers, still newer patterns for women's social guardianship.

In a popular tract written in 1885, Mrs. A.J. Graves expressed a warning against the danger inherent in over-refinement. Luxurious habits were sapping the strength of the female character, drawing women out of their true sphere. "Home is our palladium" she explained, "our post of honor and of duty, and here we must begin the work of reform." Thus practicality became the counterpart of moral greatness. But in order for women to accept this responsibility, other sources of activity had to be provided within the home. The new standards focused on women as supervisor of a renewed domestic life, responsible for quality of consumption and expanded childcare. Similarly, new standards of cleanliness arose in the Nineteenth Century, complemented by mechanical developments making housework less burdensome but not less time-consuming for the devoted housewife. Catherine Beecher, Emma Willard, and others publicized new forms of domestic science, stressing the demands of the newer business and scientific methods on woman's responsibilities. Meanwhile the influential Godey's Lady's Book mixed colorful fashions with detailed advice on domesticity. And various writers warned women against the "foreign influences" represented by the emerging servant class of Irish rather than native born women, resolving on the necessity of able women to manage without such help. (54)

In the early years of the Nineteenth Century literature addressed to women had come increasingly to focus on their motherhood, encouraging them to raise good, Christian citizens. This literature glorified the contributions mothers made to society by careful attention to the environment and potential of each child, thereby providing a career-like responsibility to the job. Theology slowly discovered children and offered a religious experience for young people different from that of their parents: Descriptions of their experience and the expectations set for them became less strict, and the Calvinist stress on their original sin was replaced by notions of childhood innocence. The psychology of John Locke and the pedagogues following him was transferred into popular writings about children, popularizing the impressionability of the human at birth and the need to implant the best hopes for each child and to discover the individual potential for each. These ideas were sharpened and their consequences for women deepened by the growing dichotomy established between men and women. Between passion and sensibility, mind and heart, the abstract and absent father and the leisured and confined mother, the gaps grew enormously. Women came to be viewed as peculiarly suited by nature and training to care for infants and their needs in the home. Culture was considered a feminine province in the world at large, but within each family respect for culture and communication of values was directly manifested by the relations between mother and child. The biological function of motherhood became elevated into a sophisticated and future-oriented definition of woman's social impact. The growing set of ideas with a wide range of detail about home, food, health, toys, clothing, and religious training was disseminated almost universally in sermons, women's magazines, books, and newspapers. (55)

Meanwhile, special schools had been established, such as Mount Holyoke in 1837, for the purposes of domestic science and the care and teaching of children. The very existence of these schools helped to legitimatize women's education, and led to the establishment of the first true women's colleges, such as Vassar in 1867. Women who graduated from the colleges or the transformed special schools became the first professionals and many of the leading feminists of the late Nineteenth Century. Thus, the concern for rationalizing women's domestic role had at last been transformed, in part at least, to its opposite. Woman's moral guardianship was re-interpreted by such reformers as Florence Kelley and Vida Scudder to be responsibility for influencing the organic evolution of society. (56)


By mid-century, women's roles in the modern class structure of America were becoming clear. The needs of the increasingly complex society called into existence a new middle class of doctors, lawyers, and other professionals. In the main, women attained this status vicariously through marriage; but in part, women too shared in the increase of opportunities for direct upward mobility through a variety of experiences and institutions including women's colleges. At the same time, a proletarianization process began on a wide scale for formerly rural populations, urban dwellers, and new immigrants. Here too women were for the most part wives, but with increasing frequency industrial workers for at least a portion of their lives.

At the beginning of industrial capitalism in America, women constituted a basic industrial work-force. As early as 1775, women had been employed during the first widespread use of spinning jennies. Government officials and entrepreneurs alike assumed women were the best candidates for service in this promising sector, in part because work in the developing textile industry involved no encroachment on traditional male-dominated trades or crafts. Women were similarly encouraged to enter early factories because their presence as a surplus labor force allowed men and boys to labor in agricultural production or in the exploration of the West. The first women workers were typically recruited from the town poor-roles, and for several decades thereafter orphans, widows, and unmarried women formed the ranks of the unskilled industrial laborers. (57)

New England textile mills provided the first opportunity for large numbers of women to work outside their immediate families in non-domestic labor. By the 1820s and 1830s, thousands of young women were attracted by the lure of the factory as an alternative to patriarchical farm life, and they traveled to the company towns of Massachusetts and Rhode Island searching employment. On the other hand, due to the migration of young men to the West, Eastern women between the ages of fifteen and thirty greatly outnumbered their male counterparts and were forced to provide their own living as single working girls. Thus the choice for factory labor was, for many, more apparent than real, especially when faced with the alternative of servitude in a brother's family. Moreover, the prevailing secondary value attached to woman's work restricted women from receiving an education or training to enable them to compete in professional or skilled occupations. Nevertheless, their preference for self-sufficiency obscured this discrepancy, and women competed with one another to gain entry into these new occupations. (58)

The early mills commonly operated under the Waltham system, a form of paternalism which provided the women with boarding houses and a strict code of moral conduct. Despite the lack of individual freedom, the mill environment offered a chance to live in a community of women, to accumulate a small savings from earnings, and to set a pattern for independent living. Although the hours were long, the work was not essentially hard, involving comparatively much free time and allowing the operative a chance for conversation and companionship. The first factories had not yet systematized the work process, and therefore production — although often experimental, sporadic, and irregular — had not yet been integrated into a rational routine of labor. Consequently the discipline of the wage-earner was far from complete. The early strikes were usually spontaneous outbursts against announcements (or even rumors) of changed policies: wage-cuts, speed ups, or lengthening of hours. Most important, this semi-agricultural factory population could respond to intolerable changes in working conditions and periods of unemployment by returning to the family farm. (59)

These first mills attracted attention for their superficially idyllic conditions. European visitors who were familiar with the grim plight characteristic of British textile industries marveled over the quaint towns operated by the mill owners and over the gentility and beauty of the young operatives. They were equally fascinated with the Lowell Offering, a journal devoted to the poetry written by the mill girls. However, these European promoters often missed the subtle fact that the Offering was published and funded by the employers to advertise their enterprise rather than to popularize the cultural achievements of their operatives. Conditions in the mills were tolerable, and wages were high enough to enable these early industrial workers to set aside a small savings. After four or five years of service, most women left the industry permanently: Some moved West where women (especially teachers) were in demand; some secured an education to set themselves on a brighter path; and others retreated to a life of alleged marital bliss.

By the 1830s, industrialism was developing rapidly, introducing new social and mechanical changes that would fundamentally alter the work situation. Technological improvements in machinery allowed greater efficiency and established the context for speeding up the work process. The new ethos of discipline destroyed the aura of gentility of earlier days, making the mill girl's position less appealing for a rising middle class of women. The depressions of the 1830s and Western competition destroyed a large number of New England family farms, forcing many daughters into a permanent factory population. Similarly, the Irish immigration beginning in the mid-1830s introduced a new class of women into the mills. Thus, while factory conditions deteriorated (more looms to tend, speeding up, more noise, dust, longer hours, et cetera) the women who entered the textile industries represented a transformed working population and took these jobs for their lives' work. Labor in the mill became a permanent experience and was no longer the first step toward a broader range of opportunities.

By mid-century, the growing work-force of women had developed an internal hierarchy. While the unskilled, industrial workers showed life styles and attitudes characteristic of the proletariat, women in the growing professions such as teaching and nursing set themselves apart from their sisters. Moreover, the dichotomy between women who worked and those who remained at home was accentuated by the culturally-defined "proper sphere" of women. Thus, while a working woman of colonial American had been considered on her own merits, by 1850-1860 her counterpart was no longer perceived as an individual attempting to earn a living; rather, she was likely to be judged as a woman who had stepped out of her place and who had thereby invited negative evaluation from her society. (60)

Middle-class women who had gained their new leisure in part from the sweat of their working-class sisters customarily returned the favor with deprecation. Although the realization of True Womanhood was possible only as an aspiration for most women, its acceptance by the influential and educated groups in society furthered the degradation of lower-class women beyond their physical exploitation. A middle-class or upper-class woman who was privileged to work in the privacy of her own home was spared from the spectacle of her indelicacy, while her laboring counterpart was easily identifiable by appearance, dress, manner, and attitude toward life.

Working-class women were inevitably marked by their participation in activities considered masculine. They shared with men a life in the world of business, a material existence which seemed inherently lacking in virtue and purity. In a Victorian culture, class stratification was culturally broadened to divide women into The Good and The Bad. Because the American ideal of femininity was so widely held, even minor deviations from the image such as dress, carriage, speech, and manners placed lower-class girls outside the pale of respectability.

For their part, working women had only one advantage: They alone
retained a right to sexual fulfillment. But without birth control and
general sexual freedom, this right constituted a negative differentiation.
Lower-class white and black women became recognized as ideal
objects of sexual exploitation, thus preserving the most precious virtue
of the Fair Lady. Most lower-class women who entered prostitution did
so because the way of life appealed to them, particularly as an
alternative to the tedious and restrictive patterns of factory work.
Meanwhile, middle-class reformers organized into social purity
associations designed to "save" women from a life of degradation.
Reformers were usually careful to attribute the rise of the Social Evil
to the new industrial and urban order rather than to the individual
wickedness of the prostitutes, but in general ascetic sexual standards
were considered the appropriate alternative. Interest in prostitutes
was usually limited to charity orphanages and female reform schools
designed to educate lower-class children into the ethics of self-control
and repressive sexuality. For the individual prostitute, "rehabilitation"
was thought unlikely, for Victorian morality was based on a standard
which considered the woman who had lost her virginity as "ruined". (61)

With their own particular needs and desires, working women discerned only slight significance in the demands of organized middle class women. The ballot, legal rights, and other social reform issues seemed irrelevant or secondary compared to the more pressing problems of daily life. As they expressed to social workers later, they wished the "secret" of preventing contraception, and when told it was abstinence, scoffed at such a solution as unreal. They envied the leisure of women who complained of boredom in their Victorian houses. And they viewed from afar the women's educational movement, designed for those of a privileged class.

Working women shared with their men the opportunities for earning money and participating in social production. Consequently, their first expression of feminist consciousness was determined by their status as a worker. By and large, they tended to join men in the ranks of organized labor and experienced their own sense of strength and power in trade unions. During the late 1830s, factory girls became involved in the first genuine trade-union protests against the fundamental technological changes in the industrialization process. The formation of a Factory Girls Association which soon attracted a membership of 2500 marked an organizational stage which transcended the spontaneous forms of earlier protests and strikes against employers. By the late 1840s, the Lowell Female Reform Association was strong enough to buy out the Voice of Industry, a paper which had long benefitted from female participation. The Voice projected a profound critique of True Womanhood, urging its female readers to attend the meetings of the New England Workingmen's Association "without false delicacy". Thus, in 1848, while their middle-class sisters met at Seneca Falls to discuss property rights and voting discrimination, advanced factory operatives such as Sarah Bagley and Huldah Stone directed their attention to subjects of wages and hours. They realized their wages were three to four times lower than those of men working in comparable jobs due to the inferiority ascribed to their position as workers. As working women, they pronounced a total rejection of the ideal woman which prevented their full participation and remuneration in industry. They rejected notions of feminine frailty, of weakness, of social purity and moral superiority, and of passivity. (62)


Nineteenth Century industrialization and urbanization had led to a fragmentation of social relations between classes and between men and women, transforming the form and content of women's roles. From the natural association of the family within pre-industrial farm life, American women passed to newer and more specialized relationships with each other through the situation of factory labor and the growth of political and social organizations. Gentility had become a widespread ideal, but even where realizable in middle-class and upper-class homes, it was undermined by the activist re-definition of moral guardianship. Working-class women, a marginal force in the early decades of the century, were by its end beginning to discover their existence as a class and their own special problems. In the Twentieth Century these changes in women's conditions were to become fully developed, intensifying for a period those class and generational differences which separated women from each other.

ENVELOPE MAKER

Several major themes emerge in Twentieth Century women's history. First, because of the breakdown of the organic family unit in which men, women, and children shared productive economic functions, women (particularly middle-class women) became society's primary consumers. At the same time, structural changes in the economy and two world wars brought ever-increasing numbers of women into the labor force. Work for women, including married middle-class women, became respectable and desirable in the Twentieth Century. Despite dramatic changes in the social and economic conditions affecting women and altering their role in society, however, the ideological gestalt of assumptions and stereotypes concerning the nature of woman and the role she was to play in society — the Cult of True Womanhood — proved remarkably adaptable to Twentieth Century conditions. Ideas about woman's sexuality have changed strikingly in the last seventy years, but the basic traditional values associated with woman as the protector of moral values and guardian of the home which developed in the ambiance of Nineteenth Century industrialism persisted into the Twentieth Century. This traditional conception of woman's role is integrally linked to women's economic function of consumption. The mature corporate economy has depended on the consumption patterns of married middle-class women buying for their homes. The "feminine mystique" was not the creation of post-World War II advertisers, social scientists, and educators, but rather was the updated version of the Cult of True Womanhood which was in evidence throughout the Twentieth Century. Finally, most of the Twentieth Century has been marked by the lack of both a feminist movement and a strong feminist consciousness. Much has been written about the nature of women and about their fulfillment, but almost invariably it has been phrased in individualistic terms. After the decline of organized feminism with the passage of the Nineteenth Amendment in 1920, women have generally had little sense of their common difficulties and their collective power, and thus have attempted individual solutions to problems of identity, sexuality, work, and self-fulfillment.

The fact that middle-class women became America's primary consumers in the first decades of the Twentieth Century is enormously important in understanding women's recent history. The same industrial developments which broke up the organic family unit by sending men into factory employment also affected women's traditional duties in the home. What women had once produced in their own homes they now bought. By 1900 most of the items which women had customarily "put up" could be purchased as canned goods. By 1910, for example, the mass consumption economy had fully developed and technological changes greatly increased American industry's production capacity. An even greater number of products were designed for use in the home. Appliances such as washing machines and electric refrigerators came into wide use in the early years of the Twenties; electric and gas stoves followed a few years later. (63)

These structural and economic changes did not, in and of themselves, transform women's historical experience. Rather, these economic developments further altered and fragmented the relationships between men and women and between middle-class women and working-class sisters. Men and working-class women, unlike middle-class women, worked outside the home in what society deemed productive occupations. As Margaret Benston has stated, a capitalistic society honors the production of exchange value, but regards the production of use value as non-productive because it does not receive financial remuneration. Hence, because women have not been paid for the work they have done in the home, society has judged such work to be devoid of productive value. The middle-class housewife's work has been separated further from the "productive" work of men because it is essentially unspecialized and unregimented. Whereas industrial production became increasingly specialized and routinized in the late Nineteenth and Twentieth Centuries, the work women did in the home underwent little structural transformation. In addition, unlike the "real" and important world of industrial production, woman's work has been geared not to clock time, but to task orientation. This fact has made housework even more of an anomaly in a society with norms based on industrial production methods. (64)

Middle-class women have been separated from their working-class sisters also in that modern technology gave middle-class women an abundance of leisure. The maturation of the corporate economy was accompanied by a growing recognition of the fact that housework no longer needed to be a full-time occupation. Many social commentators in the first decades of the Twentieth Century described the middle-class woman's "restlessness". In the early 1920s, psychotherapists and sociologists increasingly wrote about the "nervous housewife" faced with an overabundance of spare time and feelings of inadequacy, boredom, and uselessness. Alice Beal Parsons's 1924 study Woman's Dilemma delineated the frustrations and tensions of the middle-class housewife who had nothing to do. Her analysis was strikingly similar to works of the 1950s and 1960s. Other social theorists and feminists in the early part of the century decried the middle-class woman's lack of a productive economic function. Simon Patten stated that "once the household industries gave to the staying-home woman a fair share of the labor, but today they are few and the 'homemaker' suffers under enforced idleness, ungratified longing, and non-productive time killing ...." (65) Feminists such as Olive Schreiner and Lorinne Pruette argued that middle-class women were social parasites, doomed to a symbiotic existence dependent on the more productive members of society. (66)

The middle-class woman's unused energy and tensions found outlets in the feminist movement, in social reform and volunteer activities, in psychoanalysis, and in employment outside the home. Increasingly, she defined personal liberation in terms of productive and meaningful work in the world of men. World War I marked the large-scale movement of middle-class women, including married women, into the labor force. By the mid-1960s, over a third of all married women were employed. In part, this shift was due to the role of the world wars in forcing acceptance of married women workers and making work outside the home a respectable avenue for self-fulfillment. War work, however, was generally industrial in nature and was usually regarded as a temporary patriotic duty rather than as a permanent career. This was one of the factors involved in the temporary shrinkage of the number of middle-class women in the labor force after both wars. More important than the wars in changing the nature of middle-class women's employment outside the home were the structural changes in the economy which resulted in the increasing emphasis on service industries employing large numbers of "white-collar" workers. The number of telephone operators, secretaries, typists, clerks, and stenographers rose phenomenally in the 1920s, thus shaping the contours for the majority of middle-class women's employment patterns since that decade. Other well-educated middle-class women trained for careers in professions traditionally filled by men. It is interesting, however, that proportionately fewer women trained for professional careers after the Twenties than in the two decades before the First World War. In the early decades of the Twentieth Century, to train for a professional career usually involved a conscious choice to forsake marriage. In the 1920s, younger women, alienated by the older feminists' denial of sexuality, were more attracted to occupations they felt could be easily combined with marriage and children. (67)

Although an abundant amount of literature was devoted to problems facing women who wanted to combine marriage with a job, very few collective solutions were proposed. The responsibility for being able to manage what amounted to two jobs at once fell on the individual woman alone. This reliance on individual solutions to solve problems working women faced in managing a home and a job was evident even during the world wars, when the media and the state encouraged married women to work outside the home. During World War II, for instance, a propaganda tract urging women to work as a patriotic duty offered only individual solutions for the problems involved in combining two jobs. Women were told to budget their time better, move to smaller homes, and buy prepared food. (68)

Despite the fact that many middle-class women entered the labor force during the Twentieth Century, their experience differed in many respects from that of working-class women. Whether a middle-class woman worked as a file clerk or studied to be a physician, work was a consciously-made choice and an effort to find self-fulfillment and independence, not an economic necessity. Exactly the reverse has been true of the Twentieth Century working-class woman, who has entered the industrial work force because it was the only choice open to her. With the shift from industrial home work to factory machine production in the late Nineteenth and early Twentieth Centuries, an ever-increasing number of women moved into industrial employment. Such factory jobs were hardly liberating: The hours were long (often well over sixty a week in the years before protective legislation), the working conditions poor, and sexist discrimination widespread. Women generally earned about half of men's wages for the same work. In addition, women, like blacks, were often assigned tasks which were considered too degrading for white men to accept, such as scrubbing the factory floor. (69) Working women's conditions were exacerbated by the scant attention paid them by the organized labor movement. Although the American Federation of Labor passed annual resolutions calling for organization of women workers, no action was taken until well into the century. Women workers in a number of industries formed their own unions, with the help of organizations like the Women's Trade Union League, but these unions affected only a small minority. Unions considered women poor risks. Despite the efforts of groups like the Working Girls' Societies and the Women's Trade Union League to show otherwise the traditional belief that women were invariably temporary workers and the notion that a woman must only be working for "pin money" or out of selfish disregard for her familial responsibilities remained strong for many years in the Twentieth Century. Most men union organizers considered unions incompatible with "femininity". "Do they not tend to unsex them and make them masculine?" an AFL official asked Agnes Nestor, president of the women glove makers' union. (70) Thus working-class women, despite the fact that they were living contradictions to the "Cult of True Womanhood" ideal of frail, passive, and delicate femininity, suffered from the imposition of the same stereotype. (71)

Not surprisingly, working-class women who have worked out of necessity throughout the Twentieth Century have generally regarded marriage as liberation from the tedium and exhaustion of industrial employment. In addition, because working-class women have viewed work as an economic necessity and not as a kind of luxury, they have been more interested in collectively organizing to change the conditions under which they have worked rather than relying totally on individual solutions. By contrast, middle-class white-collar employees are only beginning to organize around common demands and in resistance to common forms of exploitation.

The differences in economic roles and personal expectations between working-class women and middle-class women were also reflected in the feminist movement in the early part of the century. Working-class women were generally apathetic to the goals of the organized feminist movement. They did not see the movement as furthering their collective aims of better working conditions and unionism. The National American Women's Suffrage Association, for example, was at best indifferent to the unionization of women workers, and some important suffragists were openly hostile toward organized labor. Then too, working women generally did not regard obtaining the vote as a tangible improvement in their condition, while middle-class suffragists often saw the vote as the only important goal of the movement. For them, suffrage was an end in itself. (72)

Women in the organized feminist movement accepted the economic transformation of middle-class women from co-producer to consumer and incorporated it into their thinking about their own lives and about their place in society. Some hailed woman's new role and the technological forces that had created it as the final prerequisite for the liberation of women from household drudgery. Charlotte Perkins Gilman, for example, urged that technological developments and labor saving devices be employed to liberate women from the unspecialized and inefficient ways housework was organized: Community kitchens and technological innovations would revolutionize the organization of the home and leave women free for other pursuits. Early Twentieth Century feminists combined this acceptance of consumerism with an acceptance of the Nineteenth Century ideal of woman as imbued with fixed and unchanging moral and biological characteristics and responsibilities to care for children and the home.

No longer advancing the individualistic political and legal arguments of Nineteenth Century feminism, early Twentieth Century feminists argued that women were different, morally and socially. For precisely these reasons should women be allowed to vote; the political system needed women's influence. Spokesmen in the movement constantly stressed that the home and the community were interrelated and interdependent, and that to women as buyers fell the responsibility for insuring that the work they used to perform inside the home was now performed efficiently, safely, and equitably outside it. Accordingly, women campaigned for pure food legislation and for other consumer oriented reforms. (73)

The arguments employed by organized feminism early in the Twentieth Century were not only ahistorical; they also disregarded many of the contemporary trends involving women — particularly the increasing participation of working-class women in the industrial labor force. Although some organizations within the feminist movement attempted to bridge the gap between working-class women and their middle-class counterparts, and although there was a great deal of talk about "sisterhood" within the movement, early Twentieth Century feminism remained tied to its middle-class moorings. Generally, attempts at cross-class co-operation were based on urging middle-class women to use their buying power as a way to help their working-class sisters. The consumer league movement, the union label organizations, and the women's labor groups like the Women's Trade Union League stressed that women controlled their communities' purchasing power, and thus should be knowledgeable about labor conditions. For example, middle class women were urged to insist on the waistmaker's union label when buying shirtwaists: "Now is the time for the women of New York, Philadelphia, and in fact everywhere where American shirtwaists are worn, to rise in their might and demonstrate that with them bargain hunting can be subordinated to principle and that they have said goodby to the products of the sweatshop....Friends, let us stop talking about sisterhood and MAKE SISTERHOOD A FACT." (74) But despite some earnest efforts, serious cross-class co-operation within the feminist movement failed.

The feminist movement's emphasis on the middle-class woman's consumer role, its acceptance of the basic Nineteenth Century ideal of women as morally superior to men, and its single-minded emphasis on winning the vote help to explain not only the movement's failure to reach working-class women, but also its increasing inability to move beyond its immediate goal of the franchise. By the time the Nineteeenth Amendment was enacted into law, the vote was no longer a means to an end, it was the only end most suffragists envisioned. Most of the women who had been involved in the movement turned to non-feminist political activity in organizations such as the League of

Women Voters, a group which prided itself on its lack of "feminist consciousness".

In the years after 1920 feminism as a movement and as consciousness became increasingly isolated. The fortunes of the National Woman's Party in the 1920s tell us a great deal about why feminist consciousness and a strong, organized movement declined so radically in the years after the suffrage amendment. Early in the 1920s, the NWP began to campaign for an equal-rights amendment to the Constitution, arguing that legislation was the only way to achieve equality for women. Legislation had been successful in getting women the vote; when it was apparent that the vote was not enough, what was obviously necessary was more legislation. In this sense, the NWP was a victim of functional fixedness: It saw the solution to women's role in society solely in political terms.

The NWP's single-minded emphasis on the proposed equal-rights amendment alienated working-class women and labor organizations, who viewed the proposed amendment as destructive of their efforts for protective labor legislation. (75) In addition, the NWP and feminists such as Charlotte Perkins Gilman and Carrie Chapman Catt, who lived and wrote in the 1920s, were unable to appeal to young women. The Students' Council of the Woman's Party, for example, organized in 1924, had fifteen charter members. It quickly faded away. (76) Much of the reason for the lack of appeal that the feminist tradition had for young women lay in changing attitudes toward feminine sexuality. In this respect feminists accepted the "Cult of True Womanhood" stereotype of woman as devoid of sexual needs, and thus somehow more pure. Liberation for Nineteenth Century feminists, then, included the right to abstain from sexual relations. By 1920, ideas about sexuality had changed and feminine sexuality was openly discussed. What was really "new" about the "New Woman" early in the century was not so much her desire for meaningful work outside the home as her affirmation of sexuality and her search for sexual fulfillment. In contrast, National Woman's Party members and other feminists decried the New Morality. Not surprisingly, the young women of the Twentieth Century did not respond to the traditional feminist ideology which stressed sexual repression and denial. (77)

The new ideas and attitudes about sex did not emerge suddenly. By the turn of the century, changing ideas about women's sexuality were evident in the novels of writers such as Kate Chopin, Robert Herrick, and Theodore Dreiser. The life styles of women such as Mabel Dodge Luhan and Edna Saint Vincent Millay, although their number was very small before the First World War, were indicative of social change. Freudian psychology was one of the factors which contributed to changing notions about feminine sexuality, particularly because of Freud's emphasis on the centrality of sex in human motivation. Other factors were important as well. New attitudes toward

45

feminine sexuality emerged in a larger social context of the dramatic transformation of marriage and the family. The contours of family relations have been changing rapidly throughout the Twentieth Century. In an industrial, urbanized society, a large number of children was no longer an economic asset. This fact may account for the relatively rapid acceptance which middle-class families gave to the birth-control movement. Although Margaret Sanger's early efforts in the years before World War I met with public indignation, by the 1920s young middle-class women approved of contraceptive use. (78)

The changes in ideas and norms surrounding feminine sexuality have generally been regarded by women and by students of women's history as totally liberating. For most of the Twentieth Century women have not had to endure the sexual repression that marked Nineteenth Century Victorian ideas. On the other hand, the new definition of woman's sexuality has divided women from each other throughout the Twentieth Century. With the reaffirmation of feminine sexuality, the traditional notion of sisterhood broke down. In the Nineteenth Century, many women, because they accepted the societal view of themselves as more moral, pure, and pious than men, often found emotional fulfillment in friendships with other women. Women in the Twentieth Century learned that they were expected to have emotional attachments only to men. In this way, because women competed on an individual basis for men's attention, the possibilities for women coming together to develop feminist consciousness and realize their own power lessened.

In addition, the new definition of feminine sexuality further divided middle-class and working-class women. In the Nineteenth Century, women had been divided in similar fashion, but with some important variations. The working-class woman in the previous century was not affected by many of the repressive aspects of Victorian sexuality. Working-class women were expected to enjoy sexual relations. In the

Twentieth Century, however, working-class women generally have not shared the personally liberating aspects of the New Morality. They were not affected by the tenets of Freudian psychology and the open discussion of sexual matters that the popularization of Freud's theories engendered. Often, because of religious sanctions or lack of knowledge, they have not had access to new, effective methods of birth control. Studies such as Mirra Komarovsky's Blue Collar Marriage document views on sexuality marked by fear of unwanted pregnancies, ignorance of contraceptive techniques, and often unfulfilling sexual relations. (79)

One is faced with an apparent paradox when studying Twentieth Century women's history. On one hand, ever increasing numbers of women, particularly married women, worked outside the home. In addition, for the middle-class woman at least, sexuality and the biological aspects of motherhood were no longer unspeakable topics. On the other hand, throughout the Twentieth Century, social theorists, psychologists, educators, advertising executives, and clergymen have told women that their "natural" place is in the home and that their "real" job is motherhood. In other words, the Twentieth Century has had its own updated version of the "Cult of True Womanhood".

The reason for perpetuating this traditional ideal in spite of its increasing incongruity with historical reality has been a simple one: As consumers, middle-class women have filled a vital and indispensable role in an economy based on mass consumption. In order to carry out this prescribed role, women had to be educated to accept their economic function.

The set of stereotypes and assumptions which has characterized most of Twentieth Century thinking on woman's nature and role might best be defined by Betty Friedan's term "the feminine mystique" to distinguish it from the Nineteenth Century "Cult of True Womanhood" ideal. (80) Twentieth Century thinking about women has differed from the previous century in several important respects. Although women were still taught that their place was primarily in the home, a new rationale had to be formulated to replace the obsolete reasons and theories behind the Nineteenth Century "Cult of True Womanhood". In addition, because historical changes had taken away any productive economic and social reasons why women should stay in the home, women needed to be invested with a contemporary sense of importance and productivity.

The Nineteenth Century ideal of woman was based in large part on biological arguments: Women were inferior biologically to men — they were weak, frail, incapable of strenuous mental and physical exertion. This biological "anatomy is destiny" argument was carried into the Twentieth Century in the writings of such theorists as Havelock Ellis. Ellis, in Man and Woman, expressed the view that biological differences were fundamental in determining the different social roles of men and women. He stressed that women's capacities did not "limit" her, but rather especially ordained her for certain functions. Ellis bolstered his thesis with an evolutionary biological schema based on painstaking anatomical measurements. He concluded that women were infantile types and, hence, better fitted by nature to take care of children. Ellis also theorized that women's "functional periodicity" made them vulnerable to dramatic and dangerous mood changes because they always lived on the "upward or downward slope of a curve". (81) Early in the century, Alice Beal Parsons and Leta Hollingsworth made impressive refutations of Ellis's theories. Parsons pointed out that Ellis's measurements had no statistical validity. Hollingsworth, a social psychologist, brought forth experimental evidence which revealed that women did not have a period of maximum efficiency or an emotional cycle. These new theorists stressed the importance of individual differences and concluded that women varied, just as men varied, from individual to individual. Hence one could not draw conclusions about woman's pre-ordained role from biological evidence. (82)

Strictly biological arguments could no longer be used convincingly to bolster the "Cult of True Womanhood". In their place rose a new internal, psychological rationale for explaining woman's nature and justifying her traditional role in society. The Twentieth Century affirmation of feminine sexuality was essential to the psychological rationale behind the "feminine mystique". Whereas in the Nineteenth Century women were defined — and defined themselves — by careful avoidance of sexuality, in the present century women have often been defined with reference to their sexuality alone. Sexuality has been elevated above any other factor in explaining woman's nature. In one sense, this recognition of feminine sexuality has made women more similar to men: They both have been recognized as sexual beings. But because sexuality has been isolated as the only major factor necessary to explain women's motivations and behavior, women have been further separated from male-oriented society. The popular psychological construct of women as innately passive, narcissistic, and masochistic parallels the Nineteenth Century biological argument that women were innately weak and frail. Both construct a picture of woman which is fixed and eternal and bears no relation to cultural factors. Many Twentieth Century psychologists have stressed that women find fulfillment only through marriage and motherhood, and that deviation from these norms indicates psychological maladjustment. Hence, to be a feminist has meant being "maladjusted" sexually. This emphasis on individual sexual and psychological adjustment has been another important factor in the decline of feminist consciousness which has characterized the years from 1920 to the very recent present. (83)

Two societal institutions which have had a major influence on the lives of women in the Twentieth Century — advertising and education — have done much to instill the view that woman's psychological fulfillment and "adjustment" depended on her natural role in the home. In addition, both advertising and educational institutions have attempted to stress the importance of the middle-class woman's roles as mother, housewife, and consumer in an effort to invest women with a sense of productivity. Much of the advertising directed to women in the Twentieth Century, for example, has attempted semantically to turn consumption into production. The housewife managing her home has been compared to the businessman running his firm. "Through her dealings as business manager of the home," one advertisement in the 1920s read, "the modern woman brings sound commercial sense to bear on her judgment of a Ford closed car." "Retail buying is a productive act," wrote one praiser of the new economic order. (84)

Feminists such as Charlotte Perkins Gilman had welcomed the appearance of new appliances and technological improvements as a way to help solve the dilemma of the married woman who wanted a career. Advertisements and women's colleges emphasized that women now had time to "put motherhood first", not embark on a professional career outside the home. In the Twentieth Century homemaking and motherhood became specialized professions for the first time. At the same time that technological developments made it possible for women to spend less time at housework, cultural values demanded that they spend more time perfecting household arts.

Education for women changed in the early Twentieth Century to stress the professional aspects of woman's role in the home. Educators began to emphasize that woman's economic role was different from man's and that she should be educated accordingly. (85) Home economics and child-study courses were introduced into college curricula. It was unfortunate, thought many educators and social critics, that women's education gave the impression that homemaking required no special preparation. Preparation for homemaking as a profession was conceived to give the position dignity. Women should know how to buy and prepare food, sew, and manage a well-run, attractive home. Such thinking represented a complete shift in the original rationale for education of women, which was to give women the same education that men could obtain. Some institutions continued to emphasize educating women to break away from their traditional role, but increasingly more common in the 1920s was the philosophy that women should be educated for their traditional status rather than encouraged to change it. (86)

Hence, despite economic, technological, and social changes, the ideological assumptions affecting women have remained strikingly familiar. Throughout the Twentieth Century, society has defined women in terms of distinct and limiting stereotypes, despite those stereotypes' increasing irrelevance to changing economic and social realities. For the most part, American women in the Twentieth Century have accepted and internalized the "feminine mystique", or have reacted to it as individuals. Because women have been divided from one another on class lines, because the Twentieth Century definition of sexuality has discouraged the concept of collective sisterhood, and because in the years since the early part of the century, women, like men, have been educated to act and think in a framework of individualism, feminism has been in decline throughout most of the century. Only in very recent years has feminist consciousness re-emerged. Like the women's rights movement of the late Nineteenth Century and early Twentieth Century, contemporary feminism arose out of a larger social and political movement. Unlike the first movement, however, the present movement is attempting not only to understand and change the facts of middle class women's condition, but also to understand and surmount effects of class division and social fragmentation.

"Woman's awareness of herself," Simone de Beauvoir has noted, "is not exclusively defined by her sexuality; it reflects a situation that depends on the economic organization." In the course of three and a half centuries, that awareness was reflected through the prisms of a new and labor-scarce colonial society, a transitional Victorian industrializing society, and a commodity-rich but labor-alienated modern Capitalist society. There has been no single definition of woman, but rather a succession of definitions in which self-conscious feminism has been provoked, transformed or suppressed, and provoked again. At the epochally Last Moment of the current order, the self-consciousness has gained new heights and promises to reach still further. Yet, for this to happen, women must comprehend the interior and exterior worlds of that growth, both the heightened perceptions of self and the heightened contradictions of a society whose most basic problems remain unresolved (and, to that degree, endanger all of women's progress). It is hoped that this essay will have made some small positive contribution to that comprehension. ◿

# ••• Footnotes

1. Mary Beard: WOMAN AS FORCE IN HISTORY (New York, 1946). For a discussion of Beard's use of history and critique of feminism see Berenice Carroll: "Mary Beard's WOMAN AS FORCE IN HISTORY: A Critique", MASSACHUSETTS REVIEW, XII (1972), 125-143.

2. Branka Magas: "Sex Politics: Class Politics", NEW LEFT REVIEW, Number 66 (March-April, 1971), 89.

3. Philippe Aries: CENTURIES OF CHILDHOOD: A SOCIAL HISTORY OF FAMILY LIFE, translated by Robert Baldick (New York, 1962). See also Peter Laslett: "The Comparative History of Household and Family", JOURNAL OF SOCIAL HISTORY, IV (Fall 1970), 75-87, on the nuclear family extending into pre-industrial society.

In general we are indebted to Branka Magas: "Sex Politics: Class Politics", previously cited, and Gerda Lerner for their critiques of the oppression model as a framework for women's history. See especially Gerda Lerner: "New Approaches to the Study of Women in American History", JOURNAL OF SOCIAL HISTORY, XXX (Fall 1969), 53-62. For a good example of one of the first efforts to integrate the history of American women into American social and economic development, see Carl Degler: "Revolution Without Ideology: The Changing Place of Women in America", in Robert Jay Lifton (editor): THE WOMAN IN AMERICA (Boston, 1964).

4. Simone de Beauvoir: THE SECOND SEX (Modern Library edition, New York, 1969), Page 129.

5. Eleanor Flexner: CENTURY OF STRUGGLE: THE WOMAN'S RIGHTS MOVEMENT IN THE UNITED STATES (New York, 1968); Mildred Adams: THE RIGHT TO BE PEOPLE (Philadelphia, 1967). Other studies which concentrate chiefly on the suffrage movement are Abbie Graham; LADIES IN REVOLT (New York, 1934), Olivia E. Coolidge: WOMEN'S RIGHTS: THE SUFFRAGE MOVEMENT IN AMERICA, 1848-1920 (New York, 1966), and Emily Taft Douglas: REMEMBER THE LADIES (New York, 1966). Over one half of Eleanor Flexner's CENTURY OF STRUGGLE, probably the best known and most widely read general study of American women, is devoted to the suffrage campaign, and the last quarter of the book is devoted to the twelve years before the vote was won. Flexner's work is a detailed and valuable narrative study of the women's-rights movement from its beginnings in the abolitionist movement through the ratifica-

tion of the Nineteenth Amendment. Flexner recognizes the importance of events and developments outside the scope of the movement, but, generally speaking, these aspects of women's history gain significance in her book only through their relation to the suffrage movement. The chapter on working women, for example, deals with working women's participation in the movement. Mildred Adams' THE RIGHT TO BE PEOPLE is also a narrative account of the women's-rights movement, but with an even heavier emphasis on the suffrage campaign. Like Flexner, Adams gives a detailed account of factional struggles within the suffrage movement and a year-by-year account of the fight for the vote.

6. Elizabeth Cady Stanton, Mathilda J. Gage, Susan B. Anthony (editors): THE HISTORY OF WOMAN SUFFRAGE (six volumes, New York, 1969); Carrie Chapman Catt: WOMAN SUFFRAGE AND POLITICS: THE INNER STORY OF THE SUFFRAGE MOVEMENT (New York, 1926).

7. Belle Squire: THE WOMAN MOVEMENT IN AMERICA (Chicago, 1911), Page 285.

8. Mildred Adams: THE RIGHT TO BE PEOPLE, Page 3.

9. Aileen Kraditor: THE IDEAS OF THE WOMAN SUFFRAGE MOVEMENT (New York, 1965); William O'Neill: EVERYONE WAS BRAVE: THE RISE AND FALL OF FEMINISM IN AMERICA (Chicago, 1969); William H. Chafe: THE AMERICAN WOMAN, HER CHANGING SOCIAL, ECONOMIC, AND POLITICAL ROLES, 1920-1970 (New York, 1972).

10. William O'Neill: "Feminism as a Radical Ideology", in Alfred Young (editor): DISSENT (De Kalb, Illinois, 1968).

11. See, for example, Ferdinand Lundberg and Maryna Farnham: MODERN WOMAN : THE LOST SEX (New York, 1947). Christopher Lasch, THE NEW RADICALISM IN AMERICA (New York, 1965) also employs psychoanalytic theory.

12. Edmund S. Morgan: THE PURITAN FAMILY: RELIGION AND DOMESTIC RELATIONS IN SEVENTEENTH-CENTURY NEW ENGLAND (New Haven, 1948); Bernard Wishy: THE CHILD AND THE REPUBLIC (Philadelphia, 1967); Margaret Benson: WOMEN IN EIGHTEENTH CENTURY AMERICA: A STUDY OF OPINION AND SOCIAL USAGE (New York, 1935) is another good example of prescriptive history.

13. Julia Spruill: WOMEN'S LIFE AND WORK IN THE SOUTHERN COLONIES (Chapel Hill, 1928); Elisabeth Dexter: COLONIAL WOMEN OF AFFAIRS: WOMEN IN BUSINESS AND THE PROFESSIONS IN AMERICA BEFORE 1776 (Boston, 1931, revised edition); Edith Abbott: WOMEN IN INDUSTRY (New York, 1910).

14. See, for example, Gerda Lerner: "The Lady and the Mill Girl: Changes in the Status of Women in the Age of Jackson: MIDCONTINENT AMERICAN STUDIES JOURNAL, X (1969). Also see Carl Degler: "Revolution Without Ideology", previously cited, and Nancy Cott (editor): ROOT OF BITTERNESS (New York, 1972).

15. Gerda Lerner: THE GRIMKE SISTERS FROM SOUTH CAROLINA (Boston, 1967); Margaret George: ONE WOMAN'S SITUATION (Urbana, Illinois, 1970); David Kennedy: BIRTH CONTROL IN AMERICA: THE CAREER OF MARGARET SANGER (New Haven, 1970).

16. Virginia McLaughlin: "Patterns of Work and Family Organization: Buffalo's Italians", JOURNAL OF INTERDISCIPLINARY HISTORY, II (Autumn 1971).

17. Rebecca Harding Davis: LIFE IN THE IRON MILLS (Old Westbury, New York, The Feminist Press, 1972). Tillie Olsen: "A Biographical Interpretation",

p. 79.

18. See, for example, J. P. Rousmaniere: "Cultural Hybrid in the Slums: The College Woman and the Settlement House, 1889-1894", AMERICAN QUARTERLY, XXII (1970); Carroll Smith Rosenberg: RELIGION AND THE RISE OF THE AMERICAN CITY: THE NEW YORK CITY MISSION MOVEMENT, 1812-1870 (Ithaca, 1971); Gail Parker: "Mary Baker Eddy and Sentimental Womanhood", NEW ENGLAND QUARTERLY, XLIII (March 1970); Barbara Welter: "The Feminization of American Religion, 1800-1860", in William L. O'Neill: PROBLEMS AND ISSUES IN SOCIAL HISTORY (Minneapolis, 1973).

19. Cited in Eugenie A. Leonard: THE DEAR-BOUGHT HERITAGE (Philadelphia, 1965), 33.

20. Cited in Thomas Woody: A HISTORY OF WOMEN'S EDUCATION IN THE UNITED STATES (New York, 1929, 1966), Volume 1, Page 135.

21. An excellent study exists of an exception to this statement at the Moravian Brethren's settlement in Bethlehem, Pennsylvania. Gillian Lindt Gollin: MORAVIANS IN TWO WORLDS: A STUDY OF CHANGING COMMUNITIES (New York, 1967) describes the institutional development of the colonial community in comparison with its German counterpart. In a separate article, Gollin wrote a good study of the attempt to get rid of the family structure in the community: "Family Surrogates in Colonial America: The Moravian Experiment", JOURNAL OF MARRIAGE AND THE FAMILY, XXXI (1969), 650-658. This essay deals only with white women in the American colonies. Black women were rare, since most slaves imported during the period were male. And most important, they left few records which the historian may utilize. At present, no worthwhile secondary sources exist in this area.

22. Until recent years, historians concerned with long-range developments in colonial history were little concerned with social history, and those who dealt with the smaller world of women and children were oblivious to broader questions about society. Thus, throughout the books and articles available there is no integration between the home and change, between the society and individual lives. The most efficient way to begin gathering information about the period is through an extensive bibliography, THE AMERICAN WOMAN IN COLONIAL AND REVOLUTIONARY TIMES, 1565-1800 (Philadelphia, 1962), by Eugenie A. Leonard, Sophie H. Drinker, and Miriam Y. Holden. The breakdown of topics follows quite traditional and static lines: European background, heroic and patriotic activities, status and rights, role in religious life, education, and domain in the home, in productive life, in arts, and in charity. This arrangement is very helpful for gaining basic information, but does not provide a sense of the historical dynamic during the period.

Bernard Bailyn: EDUCATION IN THE FORMING OF AMERICAN SOCIETY: NEEDS AND OPPORTUNITIES FOR STUDY (1960) provides a good bibliography on education in relation to the colonial family. His essay needs substantial updating in terms of research that has followed his suggestions. A more recent and similar bibliography is in Lawrence A. Cremin: AMERICAN EDUCATION: THE COLONIAL EXPERIENCE (New York, 1970). Cremin lists the latest studies on English and colonial households which are useful for analyzing the forces affecting family growth in the New World. Unfortunately all of these studies are remarkably unimaginative when it comes to piecing together the changes for women; important family changes apparently are only between fathers and sons.

Although about England, Peter Laslett's THE WORLD WE HAVE LOST: ENGLAND BEFORE THE INDUSTRIAL AGE (New York, 1965, paperback) is useful to this discussion.

23. Edmund S. Morgan: THE PURITAN FAMILY: RELIGION AND DOMESTIC RELATIONS IN SEVENTEENTH CENTURY NEW ENGLAND (revised edition, 1966) deals primarily with the idea of, rather than the practice of, New England families, but is valuable for understanding the ideological and religious role that family played in Puritan communities.

24. Julia C. Spruill: WOMEN'S LIFE AND WORK IN THE SOUTHERN COLONIES (Chapel Hill, 1938) is the most thorough documentation of the world of women for any geographical area. Her work does not pay adequate attention to the changes within the colonial period, but is a gold mine of information. Chapter 1 of her book describes the "womanless" years in the South and efforts to import women. A supplement is Walter Hart Blumenthal: BRIDES FROM BRIDEWELL: FEMALE FELONS SENT TO COLONIAL AMERICA (Rutland, Vermont, 1962).

25. The major study of the colonial sex ratio is Herbert Moller: "Sex Composition and Correlated Culture Patterns of Colonial America", WILLIAM AND MARY QUARTERLY, Third Series, II (1945), 113-153. His statistics are helpful, but the suggestions he offers about the cultural effects are so riddled with bad psychology and with elementary sexist assumptions (such as that only frustrated single women were interested in religious revivals) that they are useless. Some changes in marriage age during the Seventeenth Century can be found in John Demos: "Notes on Life in Plymouth Colony", WILLIAM AND MARY QUARTERLY, Third Series, XXII (1965), 264-486, and Philip J. Greven, Junior: FOUR GENERATIONS: POPULATION, LAND, AND FAMILY IN COLONIAL ANDOVER, MASSACHUSETTS (Ithaca, 1970).

26. Alice Morse Earle: HOME LIFE IN COLONIAL DAYS (New York, 1899) still affords a concise treatment of household production (particularly its tools and processes) in the period. Further suggestions appear in the bibliography by Leonard, Drinker, and Holden previously cited.

27. Edmund S. Morgan: THE PURITAN FAMILY, previously cited, discusses the child-trading phenomenon in New England extensively, although his conclusions about parental fear of intimacy need revision since the work of Philippe Aries: CENTURIES OF CHILDHOOD.

David Rothman: "A Note on the Study of the Colonial Family", WILLIAM AND MARY QUARTERLY, Third Series, XXIII (1966), 627-634, reviews Bailyn and Morgan in light of Aries.

28. Anne Grant: MEMOIRS OF AN AFRICAN LADY, WITH SKETCHES OF MANNERS AND SCENERY IN AMERICA (New York, 1808, 1846), and E. W. Andrews (editor): JOURNAL OF A LADY OF QUALITY, BEING THE NARRATIVE OF A JOURNEY FROM SCOTLAND TO THE WEST INDIES, NORTH CAROLINA, AND PORTUGAL IN THE YEARS 1774 TO 1776 (New Haven, 1923). Most of Mrs. Grant's observations are more telling about the early Nineteenth Century than about the Eighteenth. Her frequent digressions on the glories of home and mother do not ring true to the pre-Revolutionary time.

29. Spruill: WOMEN'S LIFE AND WORK, previously cited; Morgan: THE PURITAN FAMILY, previously cited; and Morgan: VIRGINIANS AT HOME: FAMILY LIFE IN THE EIGHTEENTH CENTURY (Williamsburg, 1952) are useful here. Puritan attitudes toward sex and the evidence of freer practice in the late Eighteenth Century are in: Charles F. Adams: "Some Phases of Sexual Morality and Church Discipline in New England", MASSACHUSETTS HISTORICAL SOCIETY PROCEEDINGS, Series 2, VI (1891), 477-516; Edmund S. Morgan: "Puritans and Sex", NEW ENGLAND QUARTERLY, XV (1942), 591-607; and John Demos: "Families in Colonial Bristol, Rhode Island: An Exercise in

Historical Demography", WILLIAM AND MARY QUARTERLY, Third Series, XXV (1968), 40-57.

30. Ironically, the social solidarity of pre-industrial American society is illustrated by the Salem witch trials. Nearly everyone in Salem was involved in the trials. While most of the accused witches were women, there were also men; while most were white, there was also a West Indian slave. Some of the accused were destitute, but others were respected and landed members of the village. The initial accusers were young girls (many of whom lived outside their own families), but their testimony was received by the authorities and their charges were echoed by adult men and women. Witchcraft was a problem for every resident of the village, and its extirpation a collective responsibility. Within that framework, the community mobilized young and old, men and women, poor and well-to-do. Marion L. Starkey: THE DEVIL IN MASSACHUSETTS: A MODERN ENQUIRY INTO THE SALEM WITCH TRIALS (1961) and David Levin (editor): WHAT HAPPENED IN SALEM? are standard beginnings. Starkey tells a story of adolescent energy to explain the trials. Not only do we disagree with her imposition of Twentieth Century psychology on the Seventeenth Century community, but we have tried to change the focus of the event.

31. The "outstanding" women of this period have received their share of biographies, most of them terrible, but some of them providing at least the outlines of the possible differences for women of the time. Emery Battis: SAINTS AND SECTARIES: ANNE HUTCHINSON AND THE ANTINOMIAN CONTROVERSY IN THE MASSACHUSETTS BAY COLONY (Chapel Hill, 1962) needs an article of its own to describe the psychological assumptions about women which permeate the book; Battis is simply unwilling to take seriously the possibility that Anne was dealing intelligently with a religious challenge. Mary Agnes Best: REBEL SAINTS (New York, 1925) is a collection of biographies of heroic Quakers, including those women who martyred themselves in Massachusetts. Sarah Harrison was the unsung heroine who refused to swear obedience. See Edmund S. Morgan: VIRGINIANS AT HOME, Page 47.

32. Most writers on colonial children are agreed on this point. Alice Morse Earle: CHILD-LIFE IN COLONIAL DAYS (New York, 1899, 1929), Sandford Fleming: CHILDREN AND PURITANISM: THE PLACE OF CHILDREN IN THE LIFE AND THOUGHT OF THE NEW ENGLAND CHURCHES, 1620-1847 (New Haven, 1933), and Monica M. Kiefer: AMERICAN CHILDREN THROUGH THEIR BOOKS, 1700-1835 (Philadelphia, 1948). None of these examine practice, but all make their judgments on the basis of the artifacts.

33. Elisabeth Anthony Dexter: COLONIAL WOMEN OF AFFAIRS, WOMEN IN BUSINESS AND THE PROFESSIONS IN AMERICA BEFORE 1776 (second edition revised, Boston, 1931). Dexter's examples, without her concluding discussion about reasons for the decline of female careers, have been picked up by most colonial historians. Her work remains one of the only histories which try to deal with the transition into the Nineteenth Century. Her hypotheses — male codification of the law, middle-class defensiveness against immigrants, the "lady" as luxury for males with increasing wealth, and the inability of women to gain education — were suggested but not examined in relation to anything broader than the individual examples she found.

34. This discussion is based on Alice Clark's excellent study: WORKING LIFE OF WOMEN IN THE SEVENTEENTH CENTURY (London, 1919, New York, 1968). Unfortunately her insights and methods have been ignored by American historians.

35. Cited in Leonard: THE DEAR-BOUGHT HERITAGE, Page 222.

36. From an advertisement in the Pennsylvania GAZETTE, cited in Woody: A HISTORY OF WOMEN'S EDUCATION, Volume 1, Pages 227-228. The triumph of this move is discussed by Gerda Lerner: "The Lady and the Mill Girl", MID-CONTINENT AMERICAN STUDIES JOURNAL, X (1969), 5-15. Although a number of histories of midwifery in Europe exist, virtually every one is a history of male contributions to the field. A good but brief account of midwives resisting control by doctors in England is in Thomas Rogers Forbes: THE MIDWIFE AND THE WITCH (New Haven, 1969).

37. Sophie H. Drinker: "Women Attorneys of Colonial Times", MARYLAND HISTORICAL MAGAZINE, LVI (1961), 335-351.

38. Thomas Woody: A HISTORY OF WOMEN'S EDUCATION, previously cited, is the most complete collection of information on women's education. However histories of education are undergoing great changes through re-defining learning to include what occurs outside of schools and analyzing what changes are going on in the relations between members of families and social classes that induce people to formalize learning in schools. Unfortunately, very little of this rethinking has been directed toward women. Cremin, cited above, for example, ignores the problem.

39. Rush's essay is difficult to obtain; it apparently has not been reprinted since the Eighteenth Century. It is available on the microprint cards of the American Antiquarian Society and in Rush's collected essays published in 1792. Lengthy discussions of these ideas are in Woody and in Jean S. Straub: "Benjamin Rush's Views on Women's Education", PENNSYLVANIA HISTORY, XXXIV (1967), 147-157. Neither of these, however, discusses his ideas in relation to social history.

40. Ethel Armes (editor): NANCY SHIPPEN: HER JOURNAL BOOK . . . WITH LETTERS TO HER AND ABOUT HER (Philadelphia, 1935). This fascinating story includes her educational experience, her marriage, her divorce, and her Philadelphia social life. For a lengthy commentary by a young girl on the images and choices of women in the same period, see Elizabeth Southgate Bowne: A GIRL'S LIFE EIGHTY YEARS AGO . . ., with an introduction by Clarence Cook (New York, 1887). Discussions about femininity appeared with increasing regularity in American magazines and newspapers throughout the Eighteenth Century. Some of these are discussed in Bertha Monica Stearns: "Early Philadelphia Magazines for Ladies", PENNSYLVANIA MAGAZINE OF HISTORY AND BIOGRAPHY, LXIV (1940), 479-491.

41. The extent of feminism during and after the Revolution is a puzzle, in need of clearer categories of analysis and more detailed examination. Many individual women expressed discontent with the image. Mary Wollstonecraft was reprinted immediately in Boston and Philadelphia and was widely read. (For one girl's comments on VINDICATION, see Bowne: A GIRL'S LIFE EIGHTY YEARS AGO, Pages 58-62.) The novelist Charles Brockden Brown wrote two feminist dialogues in ALOUIN, available in paperback. See also David Lee Clark: "Brockden Brown and the Rights of Women", COMPARATIVE LITERATURE Series 2, University of Texas Bulletin (1922) for a summary and an assertion of his originality. Thomas Paine published a plea for enfranchisement of women, "An Occasional Letter on the Female Sex", in Conway (editor): WRITINGS OF THOMAS PAINE (New York, 1894), Volume 1. New Jersey "forgot" to include the word "man" in its new constitution. This sort of information is catalogued in a few articles, but is confused in its vague intellectual history and in hazy definitions of feminism.

42. Herbert Brown: THE SENTIMENTAL NOVEL IN AMERICA, 1789-1860 (Durham, North Carolina, 1940), Hannah Foster: THE COQUETTE (Boston, 1794). Leslie Fiedler: LOVE AND DEATH IN THE AMERICAN NOVEL (New York, 1960), especially Chapters 2-5. MEMOIR OF MISS HANNAH ADAMS, WRITTEN BY HERSELF (Boston, 1832) provides one account of a woman making a career of writing. Rush and Hannah Foster and others expressed distaste for female novel-reading in their proposals for education, but seem not to have made a dent in its popularity.

43. Karl Marx: CAPITAL, Volume 1 (Modern Library Edition), Pages 89-90. For a historical overview of pre-industrial conditions and the rise of manufacturing in relation to women, see Edith Abbott: WOMEN IN INDUSTRY: A STUDY OF AMERICAN HISTORY (New York, 1910, 1969), Chapters 1-3.

44. William R. Taylor: CAVALIER AND YANKEE (New York, 1963), 96-99 and 118-119; David M. Kennedy: BIRTH CONTROL IN AMERICA (New Haven, 1970), 40; William Bridges: "Family Patterns and Special Values in America, 1825-1875", AMERICAN QUARTERLY, XVII (Spring 1965), 3-11; C. Richard King (editor): VICTORIAN LADY ON THE TEXAS FRONTIER: THE JOURNAL OF ANN RANEY COLEMAN (Norman, Oklahoma, 1971).

45. For examples of colonial definitions see Wallace Notestein: "The English Woman, 1580-1650", in J. H. Plumb: STUDIES IN SOCIAL HISTORY: A TRIBUTE TO G.M. TREVELYAN (London, 1955), 69-107, describing some of the English Seventeenth Century elements of this image. Anne Firor Scott, in THE SOUTHERN LADY, FROM PEDESTAL TO POLITICS, 1830-1920 (Chicago, 1970), traces the continuation of this ideal of Southern Womanhood in the antebellum period. For counterparts of women's lives on the frontier, see William Sprague: WOMEN AND THE WEST (Boston, 1940) and Dee Brown: THE GENTLE TAMERS: WOMEN OF THE OLD WILD WEST (New York, 1958). Both books contain interesting contrasts with the genteel image of Northeastern urban women. See also Janet James: "Changing Ideas About Women in the United States, 1776-1825", PhD dissertation, Radcliffe, 1954.

46. Barbara Welter: "The Cult of True Womanhood, 1820-1860", in the AMERICAN QUARTERLY, XVIII (Summer 1966), fully delineates this stereotype. Fuller treatment is accorded by Glenda Riley: "Changing Image of the American Woman in the Early Nineteenth Century" (unpublished PhD dissertation, Ohio State University, 1967). See also Ronald Hogeland: "The Female Appendage: Feminine Life Styles in America, 1820-1860", CIVIL WAR HISTORY, XVII (June 1971), 101-111. A rather interesting although unfairly critical analysis appears in a rarely used source, Fred Vigman's BEAUTY'S TRIUMPH (Boston, 1966). For one of the earliest descriptions of American Victorian women, see an early work by Mary Roberts Coolidge, WHY WOMEN ARE SO (New York, 1912), which traces the notion of femininity from its origins in pre-Victorian settings.

47. Many of these restrictions closely resembled and imitated the British Victorian culture. Two useful, although sexist, sources are Gordon R. Taylor: SEX IN HISTORY (New York, 1954), and Walter E. Houghton: THE VICTORIAN FRAME OF MIND (New Haven, 1957).

48. One of the most interesting compilations and analyses of fashion can be found in Bernard Rudofshy: ARE CLOTHES MODERN? (Chicago, 1947). See also Robert Riegel: "Women's Clothes and Women's Rights", AMERICAN QUARTERLY, XV (Autumn 1963), 390-401, for a survey of feminists' responses to and description of Victorian fashion. For an excellent critique of Victorian furnishings, see Siegfried Giedion: MECHANIZATION TAKES COMMAND (Sec-

ond Edition, New York, 1949) and Harriet Martineau: SOCIETY IN AMERICA (Anchor Abridged Edition, Garden City, 1962). Thorstein Veblen: THEORY OF THE LEISURE CLASS (New York, 1899) is also relevant. Barbara Welter: "The Cult of True Womanhood, 1820-1860", previously cited, refers to Americans' reactions to British feminists.

49. Stephen Nissenbaum: "Careful Love: Sylvester Graham and the Emergence of Victorian Sexual Theory in America, 1830-1840" (unpublished PhD dissertation, University of Wisconsin, 1968) fully developed the intellectual rationales of repressive sexuality. Similarly, Sidney Ditzion: MARRIAGE, MORALS, AND SEX IN AMERICA (New York, 1953) contains much useful information on male attitudes and theories of sexuality. See also Milton Rigoff: PRUDERY AND PASSION (New York, 1971). Ironically, one of the most sexist treatments, Eric Dingwall: THE AMERICAN WOMAN: A HISTORICAL STUDY (New York, 1956), describes at length women's denial of their own sexuality. Unfortunately, Dingwall assigns to women the blame for all the ramifications of the total repressive ethic in America.

50. For a fine but early scholarly treatment, see Norman Himes: A MEDICAL HISTORY OF CONTRACEPTION (Baltimore, 1936). David Kennedy: BIRTH CONTROL IN AMERICA, previously cited, contains a most useful second chapter: "The Nineteenth Century Heritage: The Family, Feminism, and Sex", Pages 36-76.

51. William O'Neill: EVERYONE WAS BRAVE, previously cited, Pages 4-14.

52. William R. Taylor and Christopher Lasch: "Two Kindred Spirits: Sorority and Family in New England, 1839-1946", in the NEW ENGLAND QUARTERLY, XXXVI (March 1963); Keith Melder: "Beginnings of the Woman's Rights Movement in the United States, 1800-1840" (unpublished PhD dissertation, Yale University, 1965); Carroll Smith Rosenburg: "Beauty, the Beast, and the Militant Women: A Case Study in Sex Roles and Social Stress in Jacksonian America", AMERICAN QUARTERLY, XXIII (October 1971), 562-584; and Keith Melder: "Ladies Bountiful: Organized Women's Benevolence in Early 19th Century America", NEW YORK HISTORY, XLVIII (1967), 231-255.

53. Sources on feminism and women's rights are described in Part I. For specialized studies on women and abolitionism, see Samuel Sillen: WOMEN AGAINST SLAVERY (1955); Aileen Kraditor: MEANS AND ENDS IN AMERICAN ABOLITIONISM, 1834-1850 (1969); Helen M. Lewis: THE WOMAN MOVEMENT AND THE NEGRO MOVEMENT— PARALLEL STRUGGLES FOR RIGHTS (1949); and James McPherson: "Abolitionists, Woman Suffrage, and the Negro, 1865-1869", MID AMERICA, XLVII (January 1965), 40-47.

54. Mrs. A.J. Graves: WOMAN IN AMERICA (New York, 1855), 254; Elizabeth Bacon: "The Growth of Household Conveniences in the United States, 1865-1900", PhD dissertation, Radcliffe, 1959; Catherine Beecher's best work, THE AMERICAN WOMAN'S HOME: OR PRINCIPLES OF DOMESTIC SCIENCE (Boston, 1869). Also, WOMAN'S PROFESSION AS MOTHER AND EDUCATOR (Philadelphia, 1872) is useful. Helen Papasivily: ALL THE HAPPY ENDINGS (New York, 1956) traces the glorification of the common woman in the popular domestic novels of the Nineteenth Century. Other contemporary works on domesticity include: Anonymous: THE YOUNG LADY'S OWN BOOK (Philadelphia, 1832); Lydia Maria Child: THE AMERICAN FRUGAL HOUSEWIFE (Boston, 1836); Marie McIntosh: WOMAN IN AMERICA: HER WORKS AND HER REWARD (1950); Mrs. L. Abele: WOMAN IN HER VARIOUS RELATIONS: CONTAINING PRACTICAL RULES FOR AMERICAN FEMALES (New York, 1851).

55. Changes in theology and church practice are described in Sandford Fleming: CHILDREN AND PURITANISM, previously cited. The most complete intellectual history of the motherhood literature is Ann L. Kuhn: THE MOTHER'S ROLE IN CHILDHOOD EDUCATION: NEW ENGLAND CONCEPTS, 1830-1860 (New Haven, 1947). Neither book pays attention to the possible chasm between ideas and practice, but their sense of development of the ideas is quite good. The elements of the new care are discussed by Monica M. Kiefer: AMERICAN CHILDREN THROUGH THEIR BOOKS, previously cited, and in a short but provocative article by Barbara Garlitz, "The Immortality Ode: Its Cultural Progeny", STUDIES IN ENGLISH LITERATURE, VI (1966), 639-649, in which the influence of Wordsworth and the haloed child is the center of discussion. Charles Strickland: "A Transcendentalist Father: The Child-Rearing Practices of Bronson Alcott", PERSPECTIVES IN AMERICAN HISTORY, III (1969), 5-73, tells an interesting tale of a male theoretician setting rules for his wife. Although his ideas were not particularly successful, more telling is the mother's failure to transcend herself and to meet the standards of idealized warmth and understanding toward her difficult daughters. She simply could not avoid hitting her children or making speedy punishments with the pressures she lived with.

56. Thomas Woody: A HISTORY OF WOMEN'S EDUCATION IN THE UNITED STATES, previously cited, Volume 1; Eleanor Thompson: EDUCATION FOR LADIES, 1830-1860 (New York, 1947); Helen Campbell: HOUSEHOLD ECONOMICS (New York, 1897); and Albert H. Leake: VOCATIONAL EDUCATION OF GIRLS AND WOMEN (New York, 1918).

57. David Montgomery: "The Working Classes of the Pre-Industrial American City, 1780-1830", LABOR HISTORY, IX (Winter 1968). For some information on women who were wards of the state, indentured servants, or simply trained as laborers, see Edith Abbott: WOMEN IN INDUSTRY, previously cited;

Marcus W. Jernagan: LABORING AND DEPENDENT CLASSES IN COLONIAL AMERICA, 1607-1783 (Chicago, 1931); Richard B. Morris: GOVERNMENT AND LABOR IN EARLY AMERICA (New York, 1946); and A.E. Smith: COLONISTS IN BONDAGE: WHITE SERVITUDE AND CONVICT LABOR IN AMERICA (Chapel Hill, 1947). Abbott is the only one of these authors who deals particularly with women, but the others provide invaluable information about landless residents of the colonies and provide the legal history defining their lives.

58. Helen L. Sumner: HISTORY OF WOMEN IN INDUSTRY IN THE US, IX, Report of the Condition of Woman and Child Wage-Earners in the US, US Senate Document 645, 61st Congress, 2nd Session (Washington, 1911) is an invaluable source. Alice Hyneman Rhine: "Women in Industry", in Annie Meyer (editor): WOMEN'S WORK IN AMERICA (New York, 1891). Edith Abbott assessed Martineau's findings on the extent of occupations open to women: "Harriet Martineau and the Employment of Women in 1836", JOURNAL OF POLITICAL ECONOMY, XIV (December 1906). For an unusual cataloguing of the variety of jobs supposedly open to women at mid-century, see Virginia Penny: FIVE HUNDRED EMPLOYMENTS, ADAPTED TO WOMEN WITH AVERAGE RATE OF PAY IN EACH (Philadelphia, 1868).

59. Norman Ware: THE INDUSTRIAL WORKER, 1840-1860 (Boston, 1924), Chapters 5-9, has much background information on industrialism and its effects on the wage earner, with special reference to the New England mill girls. Hannah Josephson: THE GOLDEN THREADS: NEW ENGLAND MILL GIRLS AND MAGNATES (New York, 1949); Caroline Ware: EARLY NEW ENGLAND COTTON MANUFACTURE (1931). Lucy Larcom, an early operative, mentions her mill experience in her memoirs, A NEW ENGLAND GIRLHOOD (Boston, 1889), Chapters 7-11. She also composed an epic-length poem about life in the mill town, AN IDYLL OF WORK (Boston, 1875).

60. Elisabeth Dexter: CAREER WOMEN OF AMERICA, previously cited, Pages 218-225, talks about the restrictions placed on working women after the Revolution. The best analysis of class stratification in this period is Gerda Lerner: "The Lady and the Mill Girl: Changes in the Status of Women in the Age of Jackson", MIDCONTINENT AMERICAN STUDIES JOURNAL, X (1969), 5-15. For a contemporary account see Helen Campbell: PRISONERS OF POVERTY: WOMEN WAGE WORKERS, THEIR TRADES AND THEIR LIVES (Boston, 1887).

61. William Sanger: A HISTORY OF PROSTITUTION (New York, 1898) is one of the earliest attempts at an investigation and analysis of local conditions. Some interesting contemporary accounts offer insights into the prevalence and forms of prostitution in the Nineteenth Century: G. Ellington: THE WOMEN OF NEW YORK, OR THE UNDERWORLD OF THE GREAT CITY (New York, 1869), and J.D. McCabe: SECRETS OF THE GREAT CITY (Philadelphia, 1968) and NEW YORK BY SUNLIGHT AND GASLIGHT (Philadelphia, 1882). For attitudes toward prostitution, see David Jay Pivar: "The New Abolitionism: The Quest for Social Purity, 1876-1900" (unpublished PhD dissertation, University of Pennsylvania, 1965); Robert Riegel: "Changing American Attitudes Toward Prostitution, 1800-1920", in the JOURNAL OF THE HISTORY OF IDEAS, XXIX (1969), 437-452; Egal Feldman: "Prostitution, the Alien Woman, and the Progressive Imagination, 1910-1915", AMERICAN QUARTERLY, XIX (1967), 192-206. For an interesting account of the two most famous madams of the period, see Charles Washburn: COME INTO MY PARLOR: A BIOGRAPHY OF THE ARISTOCRATIC EVERLEIGH SISTERS OF CHICAGO (New York, 1934). Other sources include AUTOBIOGRAPHY OF NELL KIMBALL (New York, 1971); Theodore Rosebury:

MICROBES AND MORALS: THE STRANGE STORY OF VENEREAL DISEASE (New York, 1971); D.R.M. Bennett: ANTHONY COMSTOCK: HIS CAREER OF CRUELTY AND CRIME (New York, 1971); Charles Winick and Paul M. Kinsie: THE LIVELY COMMERCE: PROSTITUTION IN THE UNITED STATES (Chicago, 1971), Chapter 1.

62. Norman Ware: THE INDUSTRIAL WORKER, previously cited; John B. Andrews and W.D.P. Bliss: HISTORY OF WOMEN IN TRADE UNIONS, Senate Documents, Number 645, X, 61st Congress, 2nd Session (Washington, 1911); Alice Henry: WOMEN AND THE LABOR MOVEMENT (New York, 1923); Israel Kugler: "The Woman's Rights Movement and the National Labor Union, 1966-1872", PhD dissertation, New York University, 1954.

63. Ross M. Robertson: HISTORY OF THE AMERICAN ECONOMY (New York, 1964), 336, 572. See also Carl N. Degler: "Revolution Without Ideology: The Changing Place of Women in America", in Robert Jay Lifton (editor): THE WOMAN IN AMERICA (Boston, 1964).

64. Margaret Benston: "Political Economy of Women's Liberation", MONTHLY REVIEW (September 1969), and E.P. Thompson: "Time, Work Discipline, and Industrial Capitalism", PAST AND PRESENT (1967).

65. Simon Patten: quoted in Theresa Schmid McMahan: WOMAN AND ECONOMIC EVOLUTION (Madison, 1908).

66. The problem of the "nervous housewife" was discussed in a number of works in the early part of the century. See Alice Beal Parsons: WOMAN'S DILEMMA (New York, 1924); Abraham Myerson: THE NERVOUS HOUSEWIFE (Boston, 1920). Christopher Lasch: THE NEW RADICALISM IN AMERICA (New York, 1965) documents the "restlessness" of women in the early part of the century. For early analyses of woman's role as consumer, see Bertha Lucas: THE WOMAN WHO SPENDS: A STUDY OF HER ECONOMIC FUNCTION (Boston, 1904); Lorinne Pruette: WOMEN AND LEISURE: A STUDY OF SOCIAL WASTE (New York, 1924); Olive Schreiner: WOMEN AND LABOUR (New York, 1911); Julia Jessie Taft: THE WOMAN MOVEMENT FROM THE POINT OF VIEW OF SOCIAL CONSCIOUSNESS (Chicago, 1915); Thorstein Veblen: "The Economic Theory of Women's Dress", POLULAR SCIENCE MONTHLY (November 1894).

67. US Department of Labor, Women's Bureau, Bulletin Number 46: FACTS ABOUT WORKING WOMEN — A GRAPHIC PRESENTATION BASED UPON CENSUS STATISTICS (1925); and Bulletin Number 104: THE OCCUPATIONAL PROGRESS OF WOMEN, 1910-1930 (1933). More recent studies of women's employment include: National Manpower Council: WOMANPOWER (New York, 1957) and WORK IN THE LIVES OF MARRIED WOMEN (New York, 1958).

68. See, for example, Laura Baker: WANTED: WOMEN IN WAR INDUSTRY (New York, 1943) and Margaret Culkin Banning: WOMEN FOR DEFENSE (New York, 1942). The amount of material on women's war work is considerable. Works include Mabel Daggett: WOMEN WANTED: THE STORY WRITTEN IN BLOOD RED LETTERS ON THE HORIZON OF THE GREAT WORLD WAR (New York, 1918); Katherine Anthony: OUT OF THE KITCHEN, INTO THE WAR (1943); Mabel Gerken: LADIES IN PANTS: A HOME FRONT DIARY (New York, 1949).

69. Robert W. Smuts: WOMEN AND WORK IN AMERICA (New York, 1959), 88-89. Working women's experiences in industry in the early decades of the Twentieth Century are very well documented by working women themselves, social reformers, and middle-class women who worked in industry for a short time and wrote up their experiences. See Dorothy Richardson: THE LONG DAY:

THE STORY OF A NEW YORK WORKING GIRL AS TOLD BY HERSELF (New York, 1905); Grace Dodge (editor): THOUGHTS OF BUSY GIRLS: WRITTEN BY A GROUP OF GIRLS WHO HAVE LITTLE TIME FOR STUDY, AND YET FIND MUCH TIME FOR THINKING (New York, 1892); Consumers' League of New York: BEHIND THE SCENES IN A HOTEL (New York, 1922); Edna Dean Bullock: SELECTED ARTICLES ON THE EMPLOYMENT OF WOMEN (Minneapolis, 1911); Sue Ainslie Clark and Edith Wyatt: MAKING BOTH ENDS MEET (New York, 1911); Gwendolyn Hughes: MOTHERS IN INDUSTRY: WAGE EARNING BY MOTHERS IN PHILADELPHIA (New York, 1925); Hazel Ormsbee: THE YOUNG EMPLOYED GIRL (Bryn Mawr, 1927); Bessie Van Vorst: THE WOMAN WHO TOILS: BEING THE EXPERIENCE OF TWO LADIES AS FACTORY GIRLS (New York, 1903). For discussions of the settlement workers' experience, see Allen Davis: SPEARHEADS OF REFORM (New York, 1967); J.P. Rousmaniere: "Cultural Hybrid in the Slums: The College Woman and the Settlement House, 1889-1894", AMERICAN QUARTERLY, XXII (1970); Christopher Lasch (editor): JANE ADDAMS: A CENTENNIAL READER (New York, 1960). For an overview of women's entry into the work force, see Joseph Hill: WOMEN IN GAINFUL OCCUPATIONS, 1870-1920: A STUDY OF THE TREND (Washington, 1929), and Elizabeth Baker: TECHNOLOGY AND WOMEN'S WORK (New York, 1964). For a good recent analysis of the conditions under which women work, see Elinor Langer: "Women in the Telephone Company", in William O'Neill (editor): THE LONG DAY (Chicago, 1972). This book is a new edition of Dorothy Richardson's book of the same title, already cited in the original footnotes. (The Langer article is also available as a 50¢ pamphlet from the New England Free Press.)

70. Letter from Frank Carpenter to Agnes Nestor, March 15, 1908 (Chicago Historical Society, Agnes Nestor Papers); also quoted in Philip Foner: HISTORY OF THE LABOR MOVEMENT IN THE UNITED STATES, Volume 3 (New York, 1964).

71. Alice Henry's works are the best single source for women's experience in unions. See THE TRADE UNION WOMAN (New York, 1915) and WOMEN AND THE LABOR MOVEMENT, previously cited.

72. The most useful discussions of the feminist movement's relation to working-class women are Aileen Kraditor: THE IDEAS OF THE WOMAN SUFFRAGE MOVEMENT (New York, 1965) and UP FROM THE PEDESTAL (Chicago, 1968), and William O'Neill: EVERYONE WAS BRAVE, previously cited. Helen Marot: AMERICAN LABOR UNIONS, BY A MEMBER (New York, 1915) also is useful.

73. Charlotte Perkins Gilman: WOMEN AND ECONOMICS (New York, 1966) and WHAT DIANTHA DID (New York, 1910). For discussions of the middle-class base of the suffrage movement see Aileen Kraditor: THE IDEAS OF THE WOMAN SUFFRAGE MOVEMENT and William O'Neill: EVERYONE WAS BRAVE, previously cited. Good primary source material for the consumer orientation of the feminist movement is included in Rheta Childe Dorr: WHAT EIGHT MILLION WOMEN WANT (Boston, 1910) and in the materials collected about the women's-club movement. Jane Cunningham Croly: THE HISTORY OF THE WOMEN'S CLUB MOVEMENT IN AMERICA (New York, 1898) is the most readily available source. Jane Addams also was concerned with this aspect of the feminist movement. See "Why Women Are Concerned with the Larger Citizenship", THE WOMAN CITIZEN'S LIBRARY, IX (1913), and A CENTENNIAL READER (New York, 1960). See also Janet Giele: "Social Change in the Feminine Role: A Comparison of Woman's Suffrage and Woman's Temperance, 1870-1920", PhD dissertation, Radcliffe, 1961.

74. The New York CALL (December 29, 1909), Page 4 (the special shirtwaist-strike edition).

75. The most valuable source of information on the National Woman's Party is its periodical EQUAL RIGHTS.

76. EQUAL RIGHTS (August 16, 1924). Gilman's articles during the 1920's include "Toward Monogamy", THE NATION, 118 (June 11, 1924) and "Woman's Achievements Since the Franchise", CURRENT HISTORY, XXVII (October 1927). For an appraisal of the political activities of Southern women after the franchise was won, see Ann Firor Scott: "After Suffrage: Southern Women in the Twenties", JOURNAL OF SOUTHERN HISTORY, XXX (1964). See also Carrie Chapman Catt: "Suffrage Only an Episode in an Age-Old Movement", CURRENT HISTORY, XXVII (October 1927).

77. Secondary materials on the New Woman include James McGovern: "Woman's Pre-World War I Freedom in Manners and Morals", in the JOURNAL OF AMERICAN HISTORY, LV (September 1968); June Sochen: "Now Let Us Begin: Feminism in Greenwich Village, 1910-1920", PhD dissertation, Northwestern, 1967; and Christopher Lasch: THE NEW RADICALISM IN AMERICA, previously cited. 1920's issues of such magazines as THE NATION and NEW REPUBLIC have a voluminous amount of material on the New Woman. Also see Phyllis Blanchard: NEW GIRLS FOR OLD (New York, 1930), which is particularly useful for information on contemporary sexual attitudes, and Freda Kirchway (editor): OUR CHANGING MORALITY (New York, 1924). Mabel Dodge Luhan: INTIMATE MEMORIES also is a valuable source.

78. See, for example, Kate Chopin: THE AWAKENING (New York, 1899). Useful discussions of the changes in the family and marriage appear in William O'Neill: DIVORCE IN THE PROGRESSIVE ERA (New Haven, 1967) and EVERYONE WAS BRAVE, and in Carl Degler: "Revolution Without Ideology", previously cited. See also Christopher Lasch: "Divorce and the Family in America", Atlantic (November 1966). On Kate Chopin's life and work, see Jean Stafford's review "Sensuous Women: The Women of Kate Chopin", THE NEW YORK REVIEW OF BOOKS (September 23, 1971), and Per Seyerstead: KATE CHOPIN: A CRITICAL BIOGRAPHY. A number of women have left memoirs or autobiographies which are valuable sources for the life of the New Woman in the years before World War I: Mabel Dodge Luhan's three-volume memoir INTIMATE MEMORIES (especially Volume II: MOVERS AND SHAKERS); Isadora Duncan: MY LIFE; and Emma Goldman: LIVING MY LIFE (two volumes, New York, 1971). See also Goldman's essays, LOVE, ANARCHISM, AND OTHER ESSAYS. Margaret Sanger's WOMEN AND THE NEW RACE and MY FIGHT FOR BIRTH CONTROL are also valuable. For a recent biographical study of Sanger, see David Kennedy: BIRTH CONTROL IN AMERICA: THE CAREER OF MARGARET SANGER (New Haven, 1970). Two works by Floyd Dell, LOVE IN THE MACHINE AGE: A PSYCHOLOGICAL STUDY OF THE TRANSITION FROM PATRIARCHAL SOCIETY (New York, 1930), and JANET MARCH (New York, 1923, 1927), also are valuable.

79. Mirra Komarovsky: BLUE COLLAR MARRIAGE (New York, 1962) and Lee Rainwater: AND THE POOR GET CHILDREN (Chicago, 1960).

80. Betty Friedan: THE FEMININE MYSTIQUE (New York, 1963).

81. Havelock Ellis: MAN AND WOMAN: A STUDY OF HUMAN SECONDARY SEXUAL CHARACTERISTICS (New York, 1904).

82. Alice Beal Parsons: WOMAN'S DILEMMA, previously cited, Pages 11-32, and "Manmade Illusions About Women", in Samuel Schmalhausen and V.F. Calverton (editors): WOMAN'S COMING OF AGE (New York, 1931) and Leta Hol-

lingsworth: "The New Woman in the Making", CURRENT HISTORY 27 (October 1927).

83. See, for example, Helene Deutsch: THE PSYCHOLOGY OF WOMEN, A PSYCHOANALYTIC INTERPRETATION (New York, 1944); Ferdinand Lundberg and Maryna Franham: MODERN WOMAN: THE LOST SEX (New York, 1947); Marie Robinson: THE POWER OF SEXUAL SURRENDER (New York, 1959). This prevalent psychological construct has not gone without refutation. See, for example, Clara Thompson: "Cultural Pressures in the Psychology of Women", PSYCHIATRY, V (August 1942), and Mary Jane Sherfey: "The Evolution and Nature of Female Sexuality in Relation to Psychoanalytic Theory", JOURNAL OF THE AMERICAN PSYCHOANALYTIC ASSOCIATION, 14 (January 1966). The most important study of the impact of Freudian thought on America has just been published: Nathan Hale, Jr.: FREUD AND THE AMERICANS (New York, 1971).

84. Benjamin Andrews: "The Home Woman as Buyer and Controller of Consumption, THE ANNALS of the American Academy of Political and Social Science, CXLIII (May 1929), 41, and LADIES HOME JOURNAL (August 1924), 49. Much of the most useful material on women in the 1920's is to be found in the women's magazines. The LADIES HOME JOURNAL and GOOD HOUSEKEEPING had a mass circulation for the first time in the '20's; they are the best sources for studying advertising directed at women and women's role as consumers. See also Helen and Robert Lynd's classic sociological study, MIDDLETOWN. Invaluable is the REPORT OF THE PRESIDENT'S RESEARCH COUNCIL ON RECENT SOCIAL TRENDS (Washington, 1932). Chapters are included on the changing role of women, the American family, employment patterns of women, new technological developments which affected women in the home, and consumerism.

85. Willystine Goodsell: THE EDUCATION OF WOMEN (New York, 1923), 99-110.

86. Iva Peters: SOCIAL AND VOCATIONAL ORIENTATION FOR COLLEGE WOMEN (Richmond, 1926).

87. Judith Hole and Ellen Levine: REBIRTH OF FEMINISM (New York, 1971).

This pamphlet is a somewhat revised version of an article that appeared in the July-August 1971 issue of RADICAL AMERICA magazine and was subsequently distributed as a pamphlet with the footnotes updated to 1972. In the present pamphlet, Pages 1-16 have been rewritten.

The cover is by Farrel Levy. The photographs on Pages 7, 34, 39, 42, 43, 49, 50, and 58 are courtesy of the State Historical Society of Wisconsin.